Overcoming Your Fear of Public Speaking
—*A Proven Method*

Michael T. Motley
University of California, Davis

McGraw-Hill, Inc.
College Custom Series

New York St. Louis San Francisco Auckland Bogotá
Caracas Lisbon London Madrid Mexico Milan Montreal
New Delhi Paris San Juan Singapore Sydney Tokyo Toronto

McGraw-Hill's College Custom Series consists of products that are produced from camera-ready copy. Peer review, class testing, and accuracy are primarily the responsibility of the author(s).

Overcoming Your Fear of Public Speaking
— *A Proven Method*

2 3 4 5 6 7 8 9 0 HAM HAM 9 0 9 8 7 6 5

ISBN 07-043521-9

Editor: Todd Bull
Cover Designer: David M. Daly
Printer/Binder: *HAMCO Corporation*

About the Author

Michael T. Motley is a Professor of Rhetoric and Communication at the University of California at Davis. He received his Ph.D. degree in 1970, in communication, from Pennsylvania State University. He has published extensively on his research in communication, especially in the areas of psychology of language, interpersonal communication, public-speaking anxiety. And yes, he was once very anxious about public speaking.

Contents

To
two cherished professors—

Bernard Kissel
who showed me a way to deal with anxiety

and

Theodore Clevenger, Jr.
who showed me how to research it, and so much more.

CHAPTER 1

PUBLIC-SPEAKING ANXIETY—
GETTING TO KNOW WHAT AILS YOU

Most everyone gets anxious about giving speeches. For some, the anxiety is overwhelming, or close to it. Here's how one 39 year old business executive describes his experience:

> I get panicky about two weeks before the speech, and there'll be a few nights that I can't sleep because I'm so worried about it. Then when I give the speech, I feel like I'm out of control—like I don't really know what I'm doing up there. My heart is pounding so hard I actually think I'm going to burst something. All I can think about is getting it over with, and then when it's finally over, I can't remember what happened. It's like I've practically "blacked out" during the speech.

A nurse in her early 30s puts it this way:

> I just know something is going to go wrong and I'll embarrass myself in front of everyone. So I'm scared. I shake all over—my hands, my knees, my voice. It's terrible.

From a young man just starting out in public relations :

> I always get through the speech, but I don't know how, because I'm petrified. And it seems like there's nothing I can do about it. I'm giving the speech — saying what I prepared — but it feels like some sort of robot is talking instead of me; because my mind is full of a zillion disjointed thoughts rushing around about my gestures, and voice, and eye contact, and even about my nervousness; maybe especially that. I sit down feeling relieved that it's over, but not really satisfied that I've given a very good speech.

You get the idea, I imagine, and chances are that you could provide your own description from your own experience. The details might vary a bit, but the bottom line is the same: Anxiety about public speaking is unpleasant at the very least. If the anxiety is severe enough, it can interfere with our ability to give a decent speech. It can even interfere with our willingness to give a speech at all.

These days, most of us are called upon to give speeches from time to time. And the frequency of these invitations or assignments increases as we become more active or prominent in our respective vocations, communities, business and professional associations, and so forth. It makes sense that those who experience anxiety in public speaking situations wish there were something they could do about it. I'm assuming that as a reader of this book, you are one such speaker.

I am assuming also that you can indeed do something about your anxiety, and can become a confident, relaxed, and competent speaker. I can say this without knowing you personally, simply because so many others in your predicament have been helped already through the very same approach that we will take in this book.

What I want to do in this first chapter is to acquaint you a bit with the nature of the problem. Of course, your past speech experiences may have made you as well acquainted with stage fright as you care to be! But it will be worthwhile to look at the anxiety in a more detached way. A basic understanding of the problem will help to give you confidence that it can be licked, and will help you to understand the approach we will be taking to solve the problem.

YOU ARE NOT ALONE

Practically everyone—about 85% of the population, in fact—experiences "stage fright" when they give a speech. Not all of these experiences are as severe as yours, maybe, but you probably would be surprised to know how many are. Surveys show, for example, that the number one fear among American adults—ranking above the fear of snakes, heights, disease, financial problems, or even death—is the fear of speaking before a group! This is not logical, of course, since the consequences of giving a speech are rarely on a par with disease, financial problems, falls from heights, and so forth. But then, lots of things about stage fright are illogical.

It may surprise you also to realize that among those who experience extreme stage fright are persons well known for being particularly good speakers. There are stories of extreme anxiety among some of our most successful and experienced politicians, evangelists, and entertainers. Franklin Roosevelt, Ronald Reagan, Billy Grahm, Jane Fonda, Paul Lynde, Lily Tomlin, and Laurence Olivier are just a few of those reported to have suffered from extreme stage fright.

So, in terms of your own public speaking, maybe you can take some comfort in knowing that you are not alone in experiencing the anxiety. And there should be some comfort in knowing that since the fear is practically universal, it obviously does not prevent successful speeches.

Yet I'll bet you are thinking that even if a lot of successful speakers have stage fright, it would still be nicer if you could be a successful speaker without it. I agree, and achieving that goal is precisely what this book is about.

In essence, the book presents a therapy technique that has been employed successfully with hundreds of high-anxiety speakers over the past several years. I've also included a few chapters on basic public-speaking principles, geared specifically to improving your speeches—whether in the classroom or in business, professional, community, and other "real world" situations.

So that's where we're going. Let me give you an idea of how we're going to get there by briefly introducing a new way of viewing your stage fright and a new way of viewing your speeches.

SPEECH ANXIETY—WHAT IS IT MADE OF?

There is one component of speech anxiety that you are no doubt already familiar with; namely, the physical symptoms. Most individuals report some combination of signs like sweaty palms, dry mouth, increased heart rate, shaky hands, quivering voice, weak knees, shortness of breath, and "butterflies" in the stomach. With all of this going on inside, it is no wonder that the experience can be an unpleasant one. For some people it is so unpleasant that public speaking situations are avoided completely, even to the point of sacrificing success in a chosen vocation. For example, I have treated attorneys, ministers, and public-relations executives who were on the verge of quitting their professions altogether in order to avoid the anxiety that accompanied their public-speaking obligations. And I have treated others in various fields who were sacrificing their own upward mobility by passing off speaking assignments to colleagues. (All of these individuals were able to conquer their anxiety, by the way.)

The physical symptoms are just one component of speech anxiety, however. There is a second element which, though less familiar, is in some ways more important— namely, the psychological interpretation of the symptoms. A few speakers, for example, will notice an increased heart rate, or a queasy stomach, and actually interpret the symptoms as a *positive* sign of being "charged up," or "emotionally ready" for the speech. For these rare individuals, the physical symptoms remain fairly subdued and are not particularly bothersome.

It would be nice if we all interpreted the symptoms positively, but most of us don't.   Instead, we interpret the symptoms negatively.   The psychology behind this interpretation is both curious and important to understand. Physically, the symptoms are similar (though not identical) to the symptoms that occur when we experience fear. Thus, it is easy for the anxious speaker to assume that the symptoms represent fear.   But once we label an emotion as fear, we have to psychologically justify it by finding an *object* of the fear — something to be afraid *of.*   Consequently, many speakers at this point begin to imagine and invent problems that might occur should their speech be less than perfect.

These imagined consequences are almost always exaggerated and irrational. As a simple example, many speakers will claim, "It's going to be embarrassing if I make a mistake."   These individuals will later acknowledge, however, that their experience as audience members shows that audiences are in fact quite forgiving of a speaker's errors as long as the speech is generally worthwhile. And that's true, isn't it? From a rational point of view, the fear of being ridiculed for minor mistakes is obviously exaggerated.   So are almost all of the other justifications speakers invent for their fears, as we will see later.

Now, to make matters worse, the two components we have mentioned so far — the physical symptoms and the fear interpretations — can interact with one another to make a proverbial "vicious cycle:"   The speaker interprets the symptoms as fear, and invents "justifications" for the fear.

This in turn intensifies the symptoms, which then leads to even worse "fears," which also have to be rationalized, and so on. Feeding off one another, both components can escalate to the point of *extreme* physiological arousal coupled with thoughts that *catastrophic* consequences of the speech are *inevitable*. In my research, for example, I have measured heart rates of over 200 beats per minute in speakers who have become convinced that they will "make fools of themselves" during their speech!

ONE MORE CRUCIAL COMPONENT

This view of speech anxiety—physical symptoms and fear-oriented rationalizations cycling and refueling one another—has been around for many years. But it has always raised a version of the old chicken-and-egg question: which comes first, the symptoms or the imagined fears? And whichever comes first, what causes it to get started in the first place? Newer views of speech anxiety would answer that what comes first—and what gets the physical and psychological cycle rolling, so to speak, is yet another phase of public speaking anxiety. What gets the cycle rolling in the first place has to do with the *speaker's view of speeches in general*.

Specifically, most speakers with stage fright view speeches as *performances*. They view the speaker's role as that of satisfying an audience of "critics" set on evaluating the speaker's behaviors—gestures, language, eye contact, and so forth. Speakers with this "performance orientation" cannot describe with much precision just what kinds of behavior the audience-critics expect, but they assume at least that "proper" public-speaking behaviors should be rather formal and artificial—somehow "better" than their natural everyday speech.

An alternative orientation, and the one taken by many low-anxiety speakers, is the view that a speech is not a performance, but a *communication* encounter. Here, the speaker's role is to *share ideas* with an audience that is more interested in hearing what the speaker has to say than in analyzing or criticizing a performance. Notice that this creates a situation which, at least in terms of its objectives, is not very different from everyday conversation. Later we will see that it doesn't differ much from everyday conversation in terms of behaviors, either.

As for how these different perspectives affect anxiety, it happens that the performance orientation has certain anxiety-arousing associations built in. In very basic terms, it works like this: Our physical "fight or flight" response —increased adrenalin, increased heart rate, and other related physical symptoms—is triggered by all kinds of "emergency" events. One of the things that will set off this response in most any social situation is knowing (or believing) that we are going to be evaluated. Something else that almost always triggers the response is being uncertain about "proper" or "formal" behavior in unfamiliar circumstances. Since both a concern about being evaluated and a concern about "proper" behaviors are part of the performance orientation, they trigger the physiological symptoms of anxiety in public speaking just like they do in other situations.

Speech anxiety may thus be thought of as at least a three-stage phenomenon: the performance orientation triggers the physiological arousal, which in turn triggers the "fear" interpretation, which cycles with rationalizations and justifications for the fear. All of this begins well in advance of the actual speech, and continues into the speech itself. Here is a simple diagram of the process:

THE PRIMARY PHASES OF PUBLIC-SPEAKING ANXIETY

1.	2.	3.
Performance	Physical	Psychological
Orientation	Arousal	Interpretation

Performance Orientation ———> Physical Arousal <——— Psychological Interpretation

---

THERAPY APPROACHES

So, high speech anxiety apparently contains three components: 1) a *performance orientation* causes 2) certain *physical symptoms* which are 3) *interpreted through irrational justifications*. It makes sense, then, that therapy for speech anxiety should be aimed at one or more of these components. And that is just what we find when we examine successful therapy techniques for public speaking anxiety.

One popular approach, for example, concentrates on improving general public-speaking skills. The assumption is that speakers needn't be so anxious about audience reactions once they have polished their speaking skills. The jury is still out on this approach. Some have argued that while it may produce more polished speeches, it does not actually reduce anxiety. Still, the approach does seem useful for those with mild anxiety who are interested primarily in fine-tuning their speaking style.

In any case, public-speaking ability and public-speaking anxiety clearly do not go hand in hand. Some extremely anxious speakers are quite excellent (in everyone's opinion but their own), and speakers who approach the task so casually as to experience virtually no anxiety often do quite poorly. Most of us would like to "have our cake and eat it too"—that is, to get rid of our anxiety and be a good speaker. And that is why this book devotes a good bit of attention to improving your speeches. We will assume, however, that *reducing the anxiety must come first*. It doesn't do much good to know how to give an excellent speech if you're afraid to give one.

Another popular therapy approach, called *systematic desensitization*, deals directly with the physical component of speech anxiety. This approach involves training in muscle relaxation techniques, coupled with visual imagery of public speaking situations. The target is to reach a state of physical relaxation while imagining oneself giving a speech.   The assumption is that one cannot be psychologically anxious while being physically relaxed. Typically, the technique begins with the mental image of an event fairly remote from one's own speech (such as imagining being in the audience for someone else's speech). Once relaxation is achieved with that image, the relaxation process is repeated for graduated images. The finale is staying relaxed while visualizing yourself giving a speech. Although this approach is reported to be successful with many speakers, it is not the approach we will use. That doesn't mean that we will ignore the physical component of speech anxiety. We will just deal with in in different ways.

Another popular treatment approach, *rational emotive therapy*, is aimed at the mental interpretations of speech anxiety.   In particular, it attempts to get the anxious speaker to realize that many of the accompanying "fears" are irrational.   Once speakers attempt to articulate what it is that they are afraid *of*, a trained objective outsider can point out logical flaws in the corresponding reasoning, and can help the speaker toward a more realistic and less fear-oriented view of the anxiety. As a simple example, students of my public-speaking courses often report that their object of fear is the grade they are to receive on the impending speech. If this were true, then my offer to leave the room and allow the speech to remain ungraded would eliminate the anxiety. It doesn't, of course (since the fear of audience evaluation remains), and out the window goes one myth about the speaker's object of fear.   More typically, speakers will articulate irrational overgeneralizations ("I never speak well") or self-fulfilling prophecies ("I'm going to bore them to death"). Rational emotive therapy replaces such statements with more positive and reasonable ones ("I can explain my point of view to friends, so I should be able to do so with this audience," or "Since this information is interesting to me, I should be able to make it interesting to others"). Rational emotive therapy is not the primary technique employed in this book, but we will borrow some of its strategies. Throughout the book, your irrational views of what is likely to happen to you during a speech will be replaced with more realistic and less anxiety-ridden views and knowledge.

OUR APPROACH

Having discussed therapy techniques that we won't be using, let me introduce the approach that we will be using. I emphasize, *introduce*. I'll describe what the approach tries to do, but this isn't where we're going to try to do it.

By far the most successful technique I have encountered focuses on the initial component of the speech anxiety—the performance orientation. The premise is that if a performance-oriented view of public speaking is what initiates the entire cycle in the first place, then changing that view should dramatically reduce the speech anxiety. This approach operates by persuading the speaker that the goals, attitudes, and behaviors which make for effective public speaking are in fact more like those of ordinary communication encounters than of public performances. This view happens to be entirely consistent with contemporary instruction in public speaking, by the way. Once an individual genuinely approaches a speech as a communication task rather than a performance, it becomes more closely associated with daily communication episodes than with past anxiety-ridden performance experiences. Speech anxiety almost always subsides, and the speech almost always improves.

As a simple example, notice that true performances — plays, musical recitals, tap-dance routines, and so forth — usually present memorized material. When we hear a speech that sounds memorized, however, we usually don't like it. By the same token, anyone who has experienced a memory block during a performance understands one reason why true performance produces anxiety. Thus, the reason that speakers are routinely advised not to memorize speeches is that memorization *both* increases anxiety *and* produces an artificial speaking style.

Notice also that one of the goals of a "performance" is to receive from the audience a positive evaluation of one's performance skills. When this impending evaluation becomes a focus of attention, anxiety usually follows. An alternative is to focus instead on more practical goals and more realistic audience responses. For example, a jazz combo of which I am a member recently played its debut "performance." As we assembled our instruments and equipment the dominant topic of conversation was the stage fright being experienced by most of the members. But the anxiety was almost totally and immediately eliminated by suggesting that our *real* goal was not to get applause, but for the audience to have fun. And the audience would probably have fun if we had fun, so we should just stop worrying and have some fun playing our music. A nice fringe benefit was that this not only eliminated the anxiety, but in turn improved our music, I think. And it is a safe assumption that whatever "mistakes" we made were easily ignored or forgiven by the audience as long as they were having fun with the music.

The analogy for most speeches would be to recognize that the true goal is for the audience to understand the speaker's information and point of view. Thus, the main thing the speaker needs to do in the speech is simply to explain the various points clearly. It helps to recognize that, unlike our school classmates who counted the number of times we said "uh" during our book reports, the typical speech audience is more interested in hearing what we have to say than in evaluating our performance skills.

To put it another way, the preferred alternative to the "performance orientation" is a "communication orientation." This alternate view assumes that a "good speech" is one which achieves its primary communicative purpose — the audience's information-gain, attitude change, or whatever. I am reminded, for example, of a high-school valedictory address I heard a few years ago in which the speaker employed considerable oratorical flair and embellishment — fancy language, dramatic shifts in volume, practiced gestures, and so forth. It was truly spectacular. When afterward I asked another audience member her thoughts on what the young man had said, her reply was, "I really didn't understand what he *said*, but it certainly was a good *speech*, wasn't it?" The performance orientation might answer "yes," but a communication orientation would reply "no." That is, if the speaker's ideas were not received or understood by the audience, then the speech failed—no matter how eloquent the speaker might otherwise have been.

By the same token, when a speaker accomplishes the goal of sharing the intended information with the audience, then the speech is successful, regardless of how unpolished the speaker might appear upon closer inspection. Polish and eloquence have their virtues, certainly, but substance and communicative clarity are much more worthy primary objectives for the speaker. They are also less anxiety arousing.

Ironically, though, discarding the performance orientation in favor of a communication orientation actually improves the speaker as a speaker. That is to say, many of the aspects of "performance" with which the anxious speaker is most concerned—gestures, vocal inflection, facial expression, and so forth—are in fact greatly improved by abandoning the performance orientation. Most notably, high-anxiety speakers, as part of their performance orientation, are almost invariably worried about their style of delivery. Notice, however, that by far the most important quality of a speaker's delivery is *directness*—the audience's impression that they are truly being spoken *with* (rather than spoken *at*). We have all been members of audiences in which the speaker appeared to be delivering a soliloquy in some sort of far-removed oblivion. We have also been in audiences when the speaker seemed to be truly "relating"—talking directly with us and with every other individual present. Almost always, the speaker's attitude in the former situation is one of performing, and the accompanying behaviors are unnatural, artificial, and phony. And almost always, the attitude in the latter situations is one of genuine communication, accompanied by behaviors which are spontaneously natural and familiar.

For true *performances*—piano recitals, public soliloquies, and so forth—one is expected to have unusual behavioral skills, and to show them off. For *communication*, we may rely on more ordinary and natural behaviors, and certainly do not need to show them off. The gestures, vocal inflections, facial expressions, and so forth preferred in speeches are basically the same as those employed in the speaker's everyday conversation, *so the basic skills are already in the speaker's repertoire.*

The idea that public speaking is more like conversation than like performance is sometimes difficult to accept by performance-oriented speakers, but consider this: There are only two primary differences between what you do when you engage in conversation, and what you do when you give a speech: In a speech, 1) you talk longer before your "turn" is up, and 2) you get to take more time planning, organizing, and clarifying your thoughts before you speak. The advance planning is the hard part; but once that is accomplished, the actual speech presentation is the easy part.

There is one more difference between conversing and public speaking, of course. In speeches you get to share your ideas with more people all at once. It is not the size of the audience that determines whether the encounter is viewed as performance or communication, however. An exercise I have used in speech-anxiety seminars demonstrates the point: As the speaker approaches the podium, the instructor temporarily dismisses the audience, but stays to initiate a "one-way conversation" with the speaker. Basically, the speaker's instructions are to forget about giving "a speech" to an audience, and instead simply "talk" spontaneously to the instructor, using the speech-outline notes only as an organizational guide. In this one-to-one relationship the speaker will feel rather silly orating or performing, so a natural conversational directness — complete with conversational language, inflection, gestures, and so forth — quickly develops. The speaker then is instructed to maintain the conversational style while an assistant has the audience gradually return, a few at a time, so that all are present by the end of the talking. The question, of course, is at what point did the "talking" become a "speech?" Ideally, and usually, the speaker will have maintained the conversational directness, attitudinally and behaviorally, throughout. If not, then the transition from "talk" to "speech" is invariably identified by the audience as the point at which naturalness and effectiveness began to decrease, and by the speaker as the point at which anxiety began to increase. Thus, it is not the size of the audience that makes a speech a performance, but rather the speaker's goals, attitudes, and behaviors.

ROUNDING OUT THE APPROACH

There are a couple of good reasons why I prefer to gear speech-anxiety treatment toward replacing the performance orientation with a communication orientation. First, it makes sense that if the entire speech-anxiety cycle is set into motion by the performance orientation, then getting rid of that orientation would get rid of the anxiety. And if substituting the communication orientation improves the speech, then all the more reason to focus there. Second, it's not just a matter of logic or theory. I have seen hundreds of cases in which this approach has been followed by dramatically reduced anxiety and by dramatically improved speeches. Thirdly, there is impressive scientific evidence that this approach works very effectively. For example, a study was conducted at the University of California, Davis, to compare certain leading approaches to anxiety reduction. High-speech-anxiety individuals were randomly assigned to one of four groups. One was a control group that received no treatment (until after the study was completed), and a second group read a popular book on stage fright. A third group received systematic-desensitization therapy of the sort we discussed above, and the fourth group simply read the first three chapters of a draft version of this book. The first two groups experienced no appreciable change in anxiety. The anxiety of the people in the systematic-desensitization group dropped from High to Moderately High. But the anxiety of those who simply read this book dropped more than twice that much — from High to Moderately Low.

So there are good reasons to focus our attention on replacing the performance orientation with a communication orientation. But this doesn't mean that attention to the other components of anxiety is not worthwhile. In fact, since the various parts tend to go hand in hand, it makes sense that any therapy aimed at one phase of the anxiety would do well to pay a fair amount of attention to the others. Thus, while we will concentrate on replacing the performance orientation, we will not ignore the other components of speech anxiety — the physical arousal, and the irrational fears and interpretations. What we will end up with is a very complete treatment for speech anxiety.

Sometimes the complete treatment isn't even necessary. For example, many of the people I counsel can easily replace their performance-oriented misconceptions with a new communication-oriented view, and they experience a tremendous reduction in anxiety almost immediately. Let me relate a case in point — that of a young business man I met on a ski lift one day. After I mentioned during our initial "small talk" that I was a communication professor, he told me that he experienced "really bad stage fright" about public speaking. In the next fifteen minutes or so, I told him about the importance of approaching speeches as communication events instead of performances. There was only enough time to cover some of the general points

I've made in the few preceding pages of this chapter before we exchanged business cards, hopped off the lift, and skied off in different directions. That was the last I saw of him, but I received a most satisfying note a few days later about his having successfully delivered a very important speech without appreciable anxiety. The note expressed his pleasure and surprise at having been able to conquer his almost life-long speech anxiety after such a short conversation on a ski lift, saying, "It's a miracle that just thinking about getting my points across instead of 'snowing' everybody could make such a difference."

Sometimes it's that easy. Often it's almost that easy. The point is that while I don't usually do counseling in fifteen minutes, or on ski lifts, my therapy always begins with the need to change the performance orientation. Likewise, that will be the focus of this book. Some people have an easy time accepting the orientation shift. If you are one of those, you probably feel at least a little better already, and will probably feel completely satisfied well before you finish the book. Other people are more reluctant to accept the orientation shift. In those cases, my therapy goes into certain other areas. So does the book.

CHAPTER 2

SOME REALISTIC TARGETS OF
ANXIETY REDUCTION (AND SOME
MISCONCEPTIONS ABOUT ROADBLOCKS)

Serious research about public-speaking anxiety has been going on in the fields of communication and psychology since the 1930's. Hundreds of scholarly papers have been written on the subject. As is common (and necessary) in the social sciences, however, much of this research has had more to say about theory than about practical application. A standing joke to this effect circulated among communication instructors for a while. It featured a professor visited by a student seeking advice for extreme stage fright over a speech he had to deliver the following day. The professor dutifully consulted all of the available research literature and offered the only possible conclusion: "Well, based on the factors we know to be related to stage fright, you could change your sex, you could change your personality, you could get more experience, or you could change the size of your audience."

The joke was aimed at the tendency for stage-fright research to focus on factors over which speakers have little or no control, instead of focusing on things that speakers can actually do to reduce their anxiety. It happens to be true that the volumes of research on speech anxiety are generally without prescriptions for a cure. There have been several discoveries, however, which are nevertheless valuable to the anxious speaker. This chapter discusses some of those discoveries and their implications for handling speech anxiety. In some cases, the purpose of this discussion will be to dispel certain myths about anxiety — myths that are, of themselves, anxiety-arousing. In other cases, the purpose will be to understand the nature of the anxiety, so that you can realize that it is not as big an obstacle as it no doubt seems. And in still other cases, the discussion will shed light on the reasonable targets of anxiety-reduction efforts; that is, what kind of progress you can expect to make.

Speech teachers used to debate whether stage fright should even be discussed with anxious speakers. One point of view was that talking about it only makes it worse. Whether that is true depends, of course, upon what is said. The information selected for this chapter — and the same is true for the remainder of the book — is information which I have found in the past to be of considerable help and consolation to many anxious speakers.

HOW BAD HAVE I GOT IT?

It is only natural for you to assume that your anxiety, in comparison to other speakers, is extreme. Sometimes this is indeed the case, but usually it is not. A fairly reliable gauge of one's relative anxiety is provided by the questionnaire included in this chapter. You are almost bound to be curious about your anxiety level, so go ahead and take 10 minutes or so now to complete the questionnaire.

A GAUGE OF PUBLIC-SPEAKING ANXIETY*

DIRECTIONS: <u>Assume that you have to give a speech within the next few weeks</u>. For each of the statements below, indicate the degree to which the statement applies to you, within the context of giving a future speech. Mark whether you strongly agree (SA), agree (A), are undecided (U), disagree (D), or strongly disagree (SD) with each statement. Circle the SA, A, U, D, SD choices. Don't write in the blanks next to the questions. *Work quickly; just record your first impression.*

___1. While preparing for the speech I would feel uncomfortably tense and nervous. SA_5 A_4 U_3 D_2 SD_1

___2. I feel uncomfortably tense at the very thought of giving a speech in the near future. SA_5 A_4 U_3 D_2 SD_1

___3. My thoughts would become confused and jumbled when I was giving a speech. SA_5 A_4 U_3 D_2 SD_1

___4. Right after giving the speech I would feel that I'd had a pleasant experience. SA_1 A_2 U_3 D_4 SD_5

___5. I would get anxious when thinking about the speech coming up. SA_5 A_4 U_3 D_2 SD_1

___6. I would have no fear of giving the speech. SA_1 A_2 U_3 D_4 SD_5

___7. Although I would be nervous just before starting the speech, after starting it I would soon settle down and feel calm and comfortable. SA_1 A_2 U_3 D_4 SD_5

___8. I would look forward to giving the speech. SA_1 A_2 U_3 D_4 SD_5

___9. As soon as I knew that I would have to give the speech, I would feel myself getting tense. SA_5 A_4 U_3 D_2 SD_1

__10. My hands would tremble when I am giving the speech. SA_5 A_4 U_3 D_2 SD_1

__11. I would feel relaxed while giving the speech. SA_1 A_2 U_3 D_4 SD_5

__12. I would enjoy preparing for the speech. SA_1 A_2 U_3 D_4 SD_5

__13. I would be in constant fear of forgetting what I had prepared to say. SA_5 A_4 U_3 D_2 SD_1

__14. I would get uncomfortably anxious if someone asked me something that I did not know about my topic. SA_5 A_4 U_3 D_2 SD_1

__15. I would face the prospect of giving the speech with confidence. SA_1 A_2 U_3 D_4 SD_5

__16. I would feel that I was in complete possession of myself during the speech. SA_1 A_2 U_3 D_4 SD_5

__17. My mind would be clear when giving the speech. SA_1 A_2 U_3 D_4 SD_5

__18. I would not dread giving the speech. SA_1 A_2 U_3 D_4 SD_5

__19. I would perspire too much just before starting the speech. SA_5 A_4 U_3 D_2 SD_1

__20. I would be bothered by a very fast heart rate just as I started the speech. SA_5 A_4 U_3 D_2 SD_1

__21. I would experience considerable anxiety at the speech site (room, auditorium, etc.) just before my speech was to start. SA_5 A_4 U_3 D_2 SD_1

__22. Certain parts of my body would feel very tense and rigid during the speech. SA_5 A_4 U_3 D_2 SD_1

__23. Realizing that only a little time remained in the speech would make me very tense and anxious. SA_5 A_4 U_3 D_2 SD_1

__24. While giving the speech I would know that I could control my feelings of tension and stress. SA_1 A_2 U_3 D_4 SD_5

__25. I would breathe too fast just before starting the speech. SA_5 A_4 U_3 D_2 SD_1

__26. I would feel comfortable and relaxed SA_1 A_2 U_3 D_4 SD_5
        in the hour or so just before giving
        the speech.

__27. I would do poorly on speech SA_5 A_4 U_3 D_2 SD_1
        because I would be anxious.

__28. I would feel uncomfortably anxious SA_5 A_4 U_3 D_2 SD_1
        when first scheduling the date of the
        speaking engagement.

__29. If I were to make a mistake while SA_5 A_4 U_3 D_2 SD_1
        giving the speech, I would find it
        hard to concentrate on the parts that
        followed.

__30. During the speech I would experience SA_5 A_4 U_3 D SD_1
        a feeling of helplessness building
        up inside me.

__31. I would have trouble falling asleep SA_5 A_4 U_3 D_2 SD_1
        the night before the speech.

__32. My heart would beat too fast while SA_5 A_4 U_3 D_2 SD_1
        I presented the speech.

__33. I would feel uncomfortably anxious SA_5 A_4 U_3 D_2 SD_1
        while waiting to give my speech.

__34. While giving the speech I would get SA_5 A_4 U_3 D_2 SD_1
        so nervous I would forget facts
        I really know.

____(TOTAL)

To determine your anxiety score:

**1. Fill in the blank next to each "question" with the
    NUMBER printed with the response you circled.
    BE CAREFUL to enter the CORRECT NUMBER.
    NOTICE that the numbers printed with the
    responses are not consistent for every question.**
**2. Add up the numbers you recorded for the 34
    questions. The sum is your anxiety score.**

INTERPRETATION

SCORE	PUBLIC-SPEAKING ANXIETY LEVEL
34-84	Low
85-92	Moderately Low
93-110	Moderate
111-119	Moderately High
120-170	High

*Adapted from James C. McCroskey's "Personal Report of Public Speaking Anxiety," as presented in J. McCroskey, "Measures of Communication-Bound Anxiety," Speech Monographs, vol. 37.4, p. 276. Used by permission of the Speech Communication Association.

Assuming that the questionnaire results are fairly accurate, let's see what we've got. Chances are that if you scored anywhere less than "High" on the anxiety scale, you are surprised that you didn't score higher. Thus, you can take some comfort in knowing that your relative anxiety is not as extreme as you had thought, and in knowing that solving the problem will probably be less difficult for you than it is for many others. If you scored "High." or maybe even "Moderately High," then you may be feeling a bit exasperated or hopeless about the diagnosis. *Don't.* It is primarily for you that this book is written. As for whether your anxiety is so extreme that yours is a "hopeless case," rest assured that it is not. The therapy technique upon which this book is based has worked with speakers who have scored close to 170 on the questionnaire. And by "worked," I mean that it not only has eliminated the trauma of their anxiety, but also has significantly improved their speeches.

At the end of the book, the same questionnaire is repeated. I can virtually assure you that you will see a substantial reduction in the anxiety at that point. If your score on this initial questionnaire was a "bad news" diagnosis, the "good news" will be in noticing the change.

WHAT DOES IT FEEL LIKE?

The physical symptoms of speech anxiety vary from one person to the next. Common symptoms include increased heart rate, sweaty palms, dry mouth, quivering of the voice, shaking knees, trembling hands, and queasiness or "butterflies" in the stomach. It may be that you have felt all of these simultaneously during public speaking, but it is more likely that you experience some combination of a few symptoms.

Some people report that their list of symptoms seems to vary from one speech to the next. Others report having a very predictable pattern. Some people can predict not only which symptoms will occur, but also the order in which they will occur. Textbooks on public speaking used to even advise speakers to consciously anticipate and await the arrival of each symptom in sequence. The idea was that if someone had a predictable list of, say, five symptoms, then with enough speaking experiences the list would one day be reduced to four. In effect, the speaker would realize something like this: "Symptom number four, my dried mouth, has arrived, but number five, shaky hands, isn't happening this time." Realizing this progress in anxiety reduction, the speaker should feel somewhat relieved, and the list might soon be reduced to three, then two, and so forth.

Whether it is wise to consciously anticipate symptoms is debatable. On the one hand, anticipating one's past symptoms can operate as a self-fulfilling prophecy. That is to say, anticipating and dreading the onset of a certain symptom may in fact promote its arrival. On the other hand, to have not the least expectation of anxiety symptoms prior to a speech is unwise as well. The danger in this case comes from the fact that even the calmest of speakers will experience at least a few mild symptoms of anxiety. More specifically, a common situation, especially for the moderately anxious speaker, is to experience virtually no anxiety whatsoever up to the last few moments before beginning a particular speech. The problem that often occurs in this case is that the speaker incorrectly concludes, no doubt with considerable satisfaction, that the dream has come true: "I'm not feeling it yet. By golly, today I'm going to give my first speech with zero anxiety." But at some point symptoms do appear, as is practically inevitable even with relaxed speakers, and the dream is shattered. Often, the speaker who has been fooled into expecting no symptoms whatsoever is just as traumatized by the last-minute "surprise" symptoms as is the speaker who has consciously anticipated, and perhaps even conjured up, an even longer list of symptoms for an even longer period of time.

The wise advice no doubt falls in the middle of these extremes. While it may be counterproductive to consciously anticipate the arrival of each symptom, it is dangerous also to not be expecting that a symptom or two will almost certainly rear its ugly head. Do realize, however, when a symptom occurs, that it is by no means a sign that the entire anxiety cycle you have experienced in the past is about to occur again. When the symptoms occur, greet them as expected — something you knew was going to happen — not something that shocks you into an overreaction.

In case you are thinking that this advice is a version of saying that you will simply have to learn to live with your physical symptoms, rest assured that this is not the case. If you are an anxious speaker now, then as a non-anxious speaker you can expect to experience far fewer, far less intense, and far less prolonged physical symptoms, as I assume you had hoped. Almost always, however, there will be a tiny residue of one or two symptoms. But these minor symptoms are felt by even the *least* anxious speakers. These minor symptoms are so slight and so short lived that they are easy to dismiss. In other words, they are not particulary troublesome for the speaker. Let's take a closer look at this in the next section.

SYMPTOMS DURING THE SPEECH

Research on heart rate during public speaking has provided insights into what speakers of various anxiety levels experience. Some of these insights are surprising. They offer consolation to anxious speakers, suggest reasonable targets for anxiety reduction, and even hint at ways to aid anxiety reduction.

Take the case of the typical high or moderately-high-anxiety speaker. In the few minutes right before the speech begins, the heart rate has accelerated to a noticeable and at least slightly uncomfortable level. This phase of the anxiety is called the *Anticipation Reaction*, and you probably can remember having experienced it right before a speech.

Next, when the speaker gets up to face the audience and begin the speech, there is a tremendous surge of adrenalin. Heart rates can soar to extremely high and uncomfortable levels. This phase is called the *Confrontation Reaction*, and if you've ever given a speech then I know you've experienced this one. It is not unusual for speakers, when confronting the audience, to reach heart rates of over 110 beats per minute (compared to normal resting heart rates in the 70's). Some speakers exceed 180 beats per minute, which is truly astounding when you consider it. We can view the Anticipation and Confrontation phases as the "bad news." Probably it isn't really "news" at all to most speakers.

The "good news" is that there is a third phase, called the *Adaptation Reaction*. Within sixty seconds or less, the heart rate begins a gradual and fairly steady decline. The rate of adaptation varies from speaker to speaker, but for most speakers it reaches a comfortable level within a couple of minutes.

The reason I call the Adaptation Reaction "good news" is that many speakers are unaware of it. The initial Confrontation Reaction is so overpowering and so traumatic that it is the only anxiety level they notice during the speech, and the only level they remember after the speech. Even though the Confrontation Reaction lasts a relatively short while, it often becomes the basis for speakers' psychological impression of the entire anxiety experience. I have heard speakers insist that their heart rate never drops below the extreme levels associated with beginning the speech, only to be shown a print-out of their actual heart rate which demonstrates a dramatic heart-rate reduction over the course of the speech. If your image is that your anxiety *remains* at the extreme level you have experienced at the beginning of your speeches, then it is no wonder that you might be reluctant to give another one.

Just realizing that the physiological anxiety does subside during the speech should be a bit comforting, but there is actually something more positive that you can do with the information. Namely, you can monitor and *notice* the adaptation. That is to say, consciously notice the adaptation as your speech progresses. Some speakers who consciously monitor their adaptation during a speech actually accelerate their adaptation process. The effect is a sort of "I'm better already . . . better yet . . . better yet" reaction.

We have been discussing the heart-rate patterns of anxious speakers. It is worth taking a look at the patterns of low-anxiety speakers, so that you will have a realistic idea of what you should be shooting for.

Low-anxiety speakers have exactly the same phases as high-anxiety speakers—Anticipation, Confrontation, and Adaptation. There are two differences: One is that the physical reactions during Anticipation and Confrontation, while higher than normal resting states, are not as high as those of anxious speakers. The other difference is that the Adaptation phase begins earlier and the adaptation is much faster. You can get an idea of these differences from the chart on the following page.

It is probably useless to hope for absolutely no physical reaction to the speech. It just doesn't happen, at least not if the speaker views the speech as important. What we should aim for is the pattern of the low-anxiety speaker. The Confrontation Reaction occurs, to be sure, and it is naive to be surprised by it. But there is no reason for it to panic the speaker, once one realizes that it will subside. In low-anxiety speakers it subsides quickly (usually within about 15 - 30 seconds), and the remainder of the speech is virtually anxiety-free.

One other difference between high and low-anxiety speakers is worth mentioning. You may have noticed that the questionnaire at the beginning of this chapter contained questions not only about anxiety during the speech, but also about anxiety before the speech. If you are an anxious

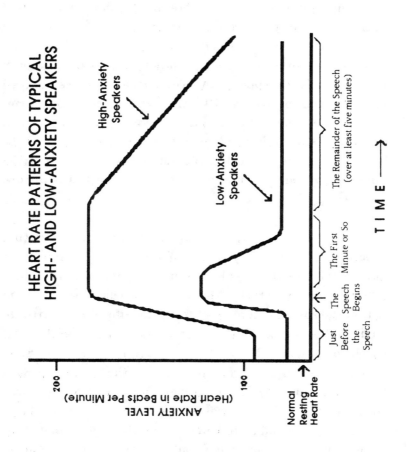

HEART RATE PATTERNS OF TYPICAL
HIGH- AND LOW-ANXIETY SPEAKERS

speaker, you probably indicated that your anxiety is experienced days or weeks before the speech is given. And as the event gets closer, the tense moments increase.

You can expect that as the ideas in this book take effect, and as your anxiety subsides, your long pre-speech agony will virtually disappear. As you become a more relaxed speaker, you probably will still experience a few brief twinges here and there, and the symptoms will almost certainly show themselves for a few seconds at the beginning of the speech. But, of course, that's nothing compared to what you have experienced in the past as a more anxious speaker.

A fascinating little experiment provides a fitting conclusion to this discussion of physical symptoms. A number of anxious speakers were randomly divided into three groups. A metering device was attached to the podium so that the speakers supposedly could monitor their heart rate during the speech. The meter contained clearly-labeled zones for "Low," "Normal," and "High" anxiety. Each speaker gave a prepared speech, and the heart rate was indeed measured by the researcher. What the speakers saw on the meter, however, was bogus, unbeknownst to them. One group was made to believe, via the meter, that their anxiety was unusually low, another group was made to believe that theirs was unusually high, and a third "control" group spoke with the meter turned off. On examination of the actual heart-rate records, the researchers found that the control group showed the same pattern as discussed above for anxious speakers. But the heart rates were much higher and lower, respectively, for the speakers falsely lead to believe that their anxiety was unusually high or low.

The moral here is that the interpretation you give to physical symptoms at one point can influence your subsequent anxiety and subsequent symptoms. Again, you should expect some physical symptoms to occur. When they do, don't assume that they are signs of your being an unusually anxious speaker, since even the calmest of speakers usually experience physical symptoms. And don't assume that once they start, they never let up, although that may well have been your perception of what has happened in the past. Rather, realize that twinges will come and go.

And don't be panicked by the anxiety surge you experience when you first begin the speech. Instead, realize that the reaction is common, even for experienced and calm speakers, and that this "Confrontation Reaction" only lasts a short while. Notice that once you are past your introduction, and "into" the speech, the anxiety has dropped off considerably, if not disappeared altogether.

There is only one way known to experience absolutely no physical anxiety symptoms prior to and during a speech, and that is to care not one iota about the quality of the speech. Obviously, that might make for comfortable speakers, but it makes for lousy speeches. While you certainly need not accept the intensities and durations of the physical symptoms you have experienced in the past, it does happen to be the case that minor remnants of those symptoms will persist as you become a calm speaker. As mere signs that the speech task is being taken seriously, these minor symptoms are good signs. But most importantly, since they are so minor compared to what you've experienced in the past, they are easy to ignore.

To summarize, the goal of the anxious speaker should not be to eliminate physical symptoms altogether, as this is somewhat unrealistic, but rather to reduce the symptoms to a comfortable level and a relatively short duration. As one sage has put it, "*The object isn't to get rid of the butterflies, but to make them fly in formation.*"

FACTORS ASSOCIATED WITH SPEECH ANXIETY

Many studies have been performed to determine the factors associated with public-speaking anxiety. Some of these factors are worth reviewing briefly. Most of them turn out *not* to be very strongly associated with the anxiety, and that serves as good news to anxious speakers.

Self-Esteem. A striking example comes from a gentleman I counseled who had read somewhere that public-speaking anxiety is associated with self-esteem. Although he was a very successful executive in a large, competitive, metropolitan area; and although he was a handsome, personable, and genuinely likable fellow; he insisted that he lacked self-esteem. I asked a number of questions about whether he felt uncomfortable or insecure in a wide variety of situations, and he answered in every case that he did not. Why then, I asked, did he consider himself to have low self esteem? His answer: "I have stage fright, so I must have poor self esteem, because I read that stage fright and low self esteem go together."

The flaw in this reasoning is that stage fright and low self esteem do not go together—at least not completely hand in hand. Their relationship has more to do with one's self image as a speaker than with self esteem in general. People who are pessimistic about their ability to give a decent speech are more anxious about speeches than those who are more optimistic. That, of course, is obvious. But knowing whether someone approaches a speech with optimism or pessimism, calm or worry, tells us very little about their general self-esteem, or vice versa.

There are lots of people with healthy general self-esteem who nevertheless experience anxiety about public speaking. The gentleman in the last example is one of these, although he had to be shown that this was the case. Like many others, he had a positive self image about almost everything *except* public speaking. By the same token, there are many people with relatively low self esteem who have confidence—or learn to have confidence—about their public speaking, and are thus low in speech anxiety. Like many of the factors to be discussed in this section, the relationship between self-esteem and public-speaking anxiety is not absolute. It is much more realistic to think of confidence about public speaking as but one tiny component of self-esteem, and to realize that this component need not match the others. You can be an anxious speaker regardless of general self-esteem, and you can become a non-anxious speaker regardless of general self-esteem. The relationship between self-esteem and public-speaking anxiety is tentative at best.

Experience. A factor which relates more directly to public-speaking anxiety is public-speaking *experience*. Generally, more experienced speakers have less anxiety than less experienced speakers. But which comes first? Do we lose our anxiety as we give more speeches, or do we give more speeches when we are less anxious about giving them? No doubt, there is an effect in both directions.

Certainly, high-anxiety individuals tend to avoid public speaking, and their level of experience tends to stay low. That is fairly obvious. What is more surprising is the lengths to which some will go to avoid speeches. There have been a number of cases of individuals abandoning an otherwise successful career altogether just because of the speeches required. As I suggested earlier, some of these individuals have even been in vocations for which the speaking obligations were predictable—areas such as law and the ministry, for example. Apparently, the perceived threat of public speaking was not realized until after they had begun their practice. Much more common than cases in which people abandon their careers, however, are cases in which people pass up opportunities for advancement because of speech anxiety. Moving up a notch in their profession or organization means that they will have to give speeches, and given the choice, they simply would rather not move up. Sometimes, the role of speech anxiety is not conscious, in which case other reasons are invented for preferring not to

advance. In many cases, though, the individual is fully
cognizant, and will readily acknowledge, that the fear of
public speaking is holding them back. Some, unfortunately,
will decide they are stuck with it; others, fortunately, decide
to do something about their fear of speaking.

In any case, the fact that high-anxiety speakers tend to
be short on speaking experience often is not because the
opportunities for experience have not been available, but
rather because they have been avoided. Does this mean,
though, that the solution to the anxiety is simply to give more
speeches? Of course not. For one thing, many anxious
speakers wouldn't be willing to take that approach even if it
did work. For another, the relationship between experience
and anxiety isn't that simple. Giving more speeches is
accompanied by feeling less anxiety only if the speech
experiences are reasonably comfortable and successful
ones. One trauma after another after another doesn't help.

Something is needed to reduce the pre-speech anxiety to
the point that at least a few speaking invitations and
opportunities will be accepted instead of avoided, and to
ensure that the experience will be a comfortable and
successful one. That is, in part, the role of any reputable
treatment program. The good news in all this is that once a
couple of successes are under your belt, it does indeed
become easier and easier. Part of a letter I received from a
once-anxious speaker makes the point:

> The first [speech] was about a month after our
> counseling session . . . . I was cool as a cucumber.
> Well, maybe not that cool, but almost. I've given

three more since then. They all went well, and one
was to a group of about 200 big shots in [my field].
There's another one coming up in a couple of weeks.
I have to get ready for it, but I'm not worried. I can't
believe what a basket case I used to be! It's so easy
now.

Effects of Anxiety Upon the Speech. As for how public-
speaking anxiety effects the speech, the answer is mostly
encouraging. Granted, there are cases in which anxiety has
caused speakers to lose control of the situation, and has
resulted in a ruined speech. But in the large majority of
cases, the speeches of anxious speakers are every bit as good
as those of less anxious speakers, all things being equal
(experience, preparation time, etc.). In fact, there is some
evidence that anxious speakers in general are better
speakers—that is, in everyone's opinion but their own.
And there is plenty of evidence that extremely high-anxiety
speakers tend to become especially good speakers once the
anxiety is controlled.

This seems at first to be counter-intuitive, but it is in
fact easy to explain. The anxious speaker cares about the
speech, and this caring—or worrying, if you prefer—often
results in planning the speech content, and in thinking
through the implications of the various choices available in
structuring and organizing the speech. Anxious speakers
rarely give speeches that are not relatively well thought out.
To put it another way, it is certainly better to be concerned
about one's speech than to be complacent about it, and most
anxious speakers are indeed concerned.

Throughout this chapter we have contrasted the state of the anxious speaker with that of the low-anxiety speaker, and the latter has been presented as the ideal target. It would be possible to try for an even lower level of anxiety — a *zero-anxiety* level. As we have seen, this target is unrealistic, since so very few speakers experience it. But that is not the primary reason it is not being advised. The very rare speaker who experiences no anxiety whatsoever almost always gives lifeless speeches, because the speech is viewed as unimportant; and gives disorganized and relatively meaningless speeches, because little or no thought has gone into the speech.

There are several stages between the time one accepts or is assigned a speaking engagement and the time one actually presents the speech — preparation of the speech, practice sessions, last-minute thoughts on the day of the speech, and so forth. The high-anxiety speaker panics or almost panics during many of these stages, and that panic often prevents efficient and competent efforts toward readiness for the speech. The zero-anxiety speaker, on the other hand, tends simply to not even think about the speech until the time comes to give it.

Somewhere between these extremes is the preferred target — the low-to moderately-low-anxiety speaker. Upon accepting a speech invitation or assignment, the lower-anxiety speaker is not panicked, frightened, or even doubtful about the success of the speech. But he or she is indeed *concerned* and involved, because success is important and it will require certain efforts. During those efforts—planning, organizing, and thinking-through the speech content—the low-anxiety speaker is driven more by a motivation to do the required work on the speech, than by a fear which inhibits or interferes with that work. Even after the work is done, the low-anxiety speaker can be found contemplating the speech during spare time—showering, driving to work, mowing the lawn, and so forth. But this is more on the order of fine-tuning than of anxious worrying.

At the extremes, the high-anxiety speaker incorrectly believes that a successful speech is beyond reach, and the rare zero-anxiety speaker incorrectly believes that an unsuccessful speech is impossible. The low-anxiety speaker recognizes that a successful speech is quite likely, but that it will require work and preparation. During that preparation there should be concern about the task at hand, but this is more positive than the complacency of the zero-anxiety speaker. It is also both more positive and more comfortable than the agony and preoccupation experienced by the high-anxiety speaker. When the actual speech begins, a momentary surge of arousal is to be expected, and there might well have been a few minor manifestations of arousal symptoms before that. Again, the fact that at least some arousal is experienced signals the absence of complacency. That the arousal is so mild and transient compared to one's past experiences signals the absence of high anxiety.

So, the realistic target is a low-anxiety state, not a zero-anxiety state. And the low-anxiety state amounts to controlled and rational responses to relatively mild twinges of anxiety—*butterflies in formation*, so to speak.

CHAPTER 3

THE CRITICAL STEP IN REDUCING PUBLIC-SPEAKING ANXIETY: ADOPTING THE COMMUNICATION ORIENTATION

In the last chapter we discussed the reasonable targets of efforts to reduce public-speaking anxiety. Now that you know what can be accomplished, let's get down to business. This chapter constitutes the main journey from high to low public-speaking anxiety.

Let's review for a moment the model of anxiety introduced in Chapter 1. The same diagram we discussed there is presented again below. Recall that when the physical symptoms of anxiety become noticeable, there is a somewhat automatic psychological need to interpret and justify them. For the high-anxiety speaker, the tendency is to interpret the physical arousal signals as symptoms of fear. Once we interpret the symptoms as indicating fear, there is a psychological need to justify the supposed fear, so we find or invent things to be afraid of—various catastrophes that may occur during the speech. These fears can provide fuel for more intense symptoms, which in turn lead to more exaggerated fears, and so on.

As for the difference between high and low-anxiety speakers, the physical symptoms are much less severe and less pervasive for low-anxiety speakers, as we saw in the last chapter. The interpretation of the symptoms is more charitable for low-anxiety speakers, as well, in part because the symptoms are relatively mild, and in part due to a set of psychological interpretations that we will discuss later.

THE PRIMARY PHASES OF PUBLIC-SPEAKING ANXIETY

1.	2.	3.
Performance	Physical	Psychological
—————>	<—————	
Orientation	Arousal	Interpretation

The primary difference between high and low anxiety speakers, however, seems to be in their overall perspective or orientation to the goals and objectives of speeches and speakers. The perspective of the <u>high</u> anxiety speaker—the Performance Orientation—happens to have fear-arousing characteristics built in as inherent components. That is to say, there are things about the way that anxious speakers *view* speeches that are almost bound to result in both excessive physical symptoms, fearful interpretations, and pessimistic prognoses about the speech. In effect, this basic orientation is what appears to instigate the cycle of physical symptoms and fear-oriented justifications.

If this is the case, then it makes sense that a reasonable approach to anxiety reduction would be to replace the orientation of the high anxiety speaker with the orientation common to low-anxiety speakers — the *Communication Orientation*. That is precisely what this chapter is designed to do. *The basic plan is simple. I am going to try to persuade you to replace your "performance orientation" to public speaking with a "communication orientation."* Some parts of this effort will be easy; other parts will be more difficult. It will be easy, for example, to persuade you, if you are an anxious speaker, that you indeed have been approaching your speeches with the performance orientation. And it will be fairly easy to persuade you that the communication orientation is much less anxiety arousing. In short, the easy part will be in agreeing that the communication orientation makes sense logically as a less anxiety-arousing approach to public speaking. You may already have been persuaded of this in Chapter 1.

The next phase is to persuade you that the communication orientation makes sense not only as an approach to reducing anxiety, but also as an approach to giving better speeches. This is easy in some cases, but it is more difficult for speakers in which the performance orientation is more deeply ingrained. Thus, a second theme running through this chapter and the next one will be the careful consideration of which orientation makes for better speeches. It is important for you to realize that abandoning the performance orientation will lead not only to more relaxed speeches, but to more effective speeches as well. Otherwise, you will be reluctant to adopt it.

As a quick example of this point, consider the following: For the past several years, public-speaking instructors within my own university, some from nearby colleges, and a few instructors of other courses in which speeches were required, have sent high-anxiety students to me for speech-anxiety therapy. After the treatment — which consists primarily of replacing the speaker's performance orientation with a communication orientation — the speaker reports substantially reduced anxiety. What is more germane to my present point, however, is that the various instructors have always reported a substantial improvement in the speeches, and the grades they assigned have reflected it.

This, it seems to me, is at least tentative evidence that the position I will advocate here — that the communication orientation to public speaking leads to more effective speeches (in addition to more relaxed speeches) — is not simply my own idiosyncratic position, but rather is shared by many others who have had a chance to directly compare the two opposing approaches.

I hope to show you how the different ways of viewing a speech affect anxiety. But in the course of doing that, I want also to show you — assuming that you are a high-anxiety speaker — that *several assumptions you are now making about what constitutes effective public speaking are simply incorrect assumptions.*

I cannot emphasize enough the importance of these opposing perspectives — the communication versus performance orientations — as the key to public-speaking anxiety. I have never encountered an anxious speaker who did not have a performance orientation, or one whose anxiety was not substantially reduced when the communication orientation replaced it. Very simply, changing your overall approach to public speaking is the key to reducing and controlling the anxiety. This includes taking a more realistic approach to the issues of what constitutes a good speech, how audiences react to speeches and speakers, and how speakers should talk and act during their speeches.

DIFFERING APPROACHES TO PUBLIC SPEAKING: THE ANXIOUS SPEAKER

As was suggested in Chapter 1, anxious speakers — most likely, yourself included — tend to approach a speech as if the objective is to put on a performance. They imagine the secret of good speaking to be a matter of following a list of specific "do's" and "don'ts," much as in performing during a music concert, or a play, or a dance recital. When it comes to public speaking, however, they usually are not certain of just what all of these various do's and don'ts are. Each anxious speaker can think of a few supposed rules — don't say "uh," don't jingle the change in your pocket, or whatever. These are anxiety-arousing, because the speaker knows (correctly) that these "rules" are easily broken, and believes (incorrectly) that breaking these rules ruins the speech. But equally anxiety-arousing is the feeling that there are other "rules" that you can't specify—rules of eye contact, perhaps, or of vocal inflection, gestures, and so forth —and that the speech is almost bound to fail because you don't know exactly what the rules are.

A useful analogy, and only a very slight exaggeration, is to say that the anxious speaker tends to view the speech much as one would view the gymnastic, diving, or ice skating performances of the Olympic competitions we have seen on television. A group of judges scores the performance, each rendering a personal verdict based on how skillfully various tiny parts of the performance were executed. Minor mistakes mean lost points, major mistakes can ruin the entire effort, and even a flawless performance may not be appreciated by a biased judge.

The anxious speaker typically views a speech in much the same way. The audience is thought of as a group of critics or judges, as if they want not so much to hear the speech as to score the speaker. The objective of the speaker, then, is like that of any performer about to be critiqued—to impress the critics. As with any performance, this translates into showing off unusual special skills. And as with any performance, "points" are gained when the various parts are executed flawlessly, points are lost when even the most minor of errors occur, and all is lost if a major error occurs. You can see how this perspective would cause anxiety.

Another way in which the perspective of anxious speakers parallels that of performances is that in both cases there is a preoccupation with the aesthetic dimensions of the task. The performance-oriented speaker tends to be preoccupied with concerns about the speech delivery. To return to the figure-skating analogy, the concern is with the "artistic impression" of the speaker in terms of delivery skills such as voice, gesture, posture, and so forth. What is especially unfortunate about this approach is that it tends to take away the speaker's freedom. Just as there is a "proper" way to perform a double axle or a pirouette, many speakers assume—incorrectly—that there is a single "proper" way to stand, talk, move, and gesture during a speech. And just as certain notes must be played in a certain order during a musical performance, many speakers assume—again incorrectly—that the words they use during a speech should be spoken precisely as written, memorized, or rehearsed.

Not only does this usually make for mechanical speeches, but it also makes for anxiety-ridden speeches. The speaker who believes that there is only one right way to give the speech knows that it will be very difficult to give the perfect performance.

ORIGINS OF THE PERFORMANCE ORIENTATION

Shortly, we will discuss an alternative to the performance orientation, an alternative in which the speaker sees the primary objective as one of imparting information, ideas, and attitudes to the audience, rather than one of displaying certain delivery skills. A large part of eliminating the anxiety associated with speaking comes in realizing that audiences are not at all like the critics of performances or the judges of performance competitions.

Speech audiences are not interested in scoring the speaker, or even in noticing the speaker's delivery skills. Rather, they are interested in hearing what the speaker has to say.   Granted, as audience members, we will occasionally notice some aspect of the speaker's delivery (favorably or unfavorably), but this is almost always secondary to our primary focus on the speaker's content. Audience members are not there to evaluate the speech; but when they do, the evaluation is based more on what was gained by *listening to the speech*, not on what was gained by *watching the speaker*. It is very important to realize this in replacing the performance perspective.

Before elaborating on that alternative perspective, however, let's take a moment to reflect upon the <u>origins</u> of the performance perspective. If it is true that speeches should not be viewed as performances, and audiences should not be viewed as critics, then why is it that so many speakers (likely, yourself included) tend to hold these views?

For most of us, there has been a sort of "conditioning" toward treating speeches as performances — a conditioning that begins with our classroom experiences in school. It happens that there are several similarities between performances and most classroom speeches, recitations, oral reports, and so forth. But it happens also — and this point is crucial — that *there are very FEW similarities between our earlier classroom speeches and the speeches we give in the "real world" outside the classroom.*   In reviewing the ways that our early classroom speech experiences tend to foster a performance orientation, notice how those experiences have been artificial in comparison to speech situations such as addressing a group of business colleagues, or the PTA, or a group of church members, a group of potential clients, or any other realistic speaking situation in which you can imagine yourself.

It is probably safe to say that in most of our early school experiences, our audience of classmates has *not* been genuinely interested in *what we have had to say.* This is clearly the case when we have had to stand and recite the Gettysburg Address, or the Preamble to the Constitution, or excerpts from Shakespeare. Obviously, the objective of these efforts could hardly be to impart information to the audience, since our classmates usually were required to memorize the same passages. (And even when they weren't, certainly the person assigning our grade already knew the material!)

It is easy to see how these early speech experiences promote a performance orientation rather than a communication orientation. First, as speakers in these classroom recitations, we are not communicating our *own* ideas. Second, the words being recited are usually in an outdated language style that is artificial for speaker and audience alike. Third, the speech material usually is already known by the audience, so we're saying nothing new. And fourth, even if there is new information in these recitations, it usually is not of any particular interest to the young speaker or to the audience.

In these cases, the speaker realizes (albeit unconsciously) that the object is not to communicate, but rather to demonstrate certain skills. At the very least, this means memorizing the recited passages correctly. Often, it means showing off other "skills" as well. There were always one or two people in my classes, for example—and probably they were in your classes, too—who would perform these routine recitations with exceptional dramatic flair. Even if the classmates groaned and regarded these performances as corny, the teacher invariably rewarded the extra effort of these students (rightly so, I suppose). And the rest of us got the idea (wrongly, I believe) that these dramatic performances are what make a good speech.

Memorized recitations are the obvious cases, but I think you will agree that the performance approach was promoted in our other classroom speeches as well. Think back to those oral book reports, for example. Some teachers told us that the object was to persuade classmates to read our book, so we ended the speech with an obligatory statement to the effect that we hoped the audience would do so. Other teachers told us that the object was to summarize the book for classmates who would not be reading it, so we summarized many pages of reading material into a few minutes of speaking as best we could. So far, so good.

But what kind of feedback did we get after those book reports—was it feedback on the clarity of our ideas, the level of interest we aroused, the desire for additional information about the book, etc.—or was it feedback on our delivery? As for feedback from *classmates*: If yours were like mine, they were much more likely to show you their tally of how many times you said "uh," or the length of time your hands were in your pockets, than to express an interest in the book. (This, by the way, probably reflects the maturity of the audience more than the quality of report. It is a rather ambitious expectation that an audience of youngsters would be genuinely interested in each of the several book reports they hear during the class period.) And as for feedback from the *teacher*: If yours were like mine, they were not nearly as likely to discuss the content of each report— asking for elaboration of important or interesting points, asking for clarification of confusing or ambiguous statements, probing the audience for responses to what was said, etc.— as they were to summarize a general list of oratorical do's and don'ts after all of the reports were finished. Granted, in book reports and similar classroom speeches there at least *could* have been a legitimate communication objective, but for many of us this focus was obscured for at least two reasons: The communicative objective was not considered to be realistically viable, and the nature of the feedback we received betrayed a performance focus by the artificial audience.

These subtle but persistent parallels between speeches and performances often continue into our later school years. Even in high school speech classes, and especially in debate, forensics, and other speech contests, it is only natural that the speaker's focus is on a primary objective other than influencing the audience—namely, the objective of "winning" a high grade or winning a contest. And on what basis are the grades or scores assigned? You guessed it! They usually are assigned on the basis of a checklist of do's and don'ts for public speaking. Granted, these checklists might include content criteria — appropriateness of the introduction, use of transitions, and so forth — in addition to the usual delivery criteria. But the emphasis is still on satisfying a checklist, rather than on whether the information is getting across to the audience.

It is easy to understand why our speeches in school were evaluated by checklists: the checklist is the easy way to grade a speech. So that you may better see what I'm getting at in this chapter, however, let me describe a less conventional but more realistic approach to grading speeches. Imagine being in a speech class, and being assigned to give an informative speech on the topic of your choice. One week before your speech you are allowed to give the class (your audience) a quiz to discover what aspects of your topic they need to hear. Then, about a week after the speech, you give the audience another quiz to discover whether they understood the main points of your speech. If they did, you get a high grade; if they didn't, you get a lower grade.

As radical as this may sound, it is precisely the approach being taken by several innovative teachers of contemporary college speech classes. The concern is with the communicative impact of the speech content, not with the aesthetic characteristics of the delivery. And the feedback has to do with factors which influenced the intelligibility of that particular speech, not with a checklist of behaviors to be performed for the sake of performing them.

This approach characterizes a *communication* orientation to public speaking. And even though you probably never experienced this approach to speech evaluation in any of your classes, *it is the one we should demand of ourselves in real-life speeches* (and in classroom speeches, for that matter). For any speech we give, we should have a clear idea of what main ideas we want to impart to the audience, and we should imagine evaluating our success primarily on the basis of whether those ideas are indeed imparted. The main reason that this helps reduce anxiety is that it focuses our attention on the organizational and other work required *before* giving the speech, rather than on our performance during the speech. As we will see later, once we have done the work necessary to make the speech clear and interesting, the actual delivery is easy.

To put it another way, ask yourself a couple of questions: Is it easier to have confidence that your speech will be perfect on every item of some unseen checklist of ideal behaviors, or is it easier to have confidence that you can get the audience to understand three or four main points of information? And if you do accomplish the communicative objectives, does it even matter whether your performance behaviors match a checklist? The answers are obvious when we realize that unlike our earlier classroom teachers and audiences, real-life audiences are not sitting out there with checklists. Adult audiences of real-life speeches are not interested in leaving with a scorecard, but rather in leaving with new information or points of view. Unfortunately, our earlier speech experiences have led many of us to believe otherwise.

A MORE REALISTIC OBJECTIVE OF PUBLIC SPEAKING: COMMUNICATION

Not all teachers promote a performance view of public speaking. In fact, the communication orientation is becoming common in college speech clases. I remember a particularly dramatic example of the communication perspective in a class I took several years ago. One of my fellow students in a public speaking class began her speech, got a few sentences into an obviously memorized performance, announced that she was too scared to continue, literally broke down in tears, and started back to her seat, sobbing and defeated. To everyone's surprise, the professor would not allow her to be seated, however, and insisted that she return to the podium. At first this seemed to be an insensitive and unsympathetic demand by the professor. But it turned out that he knew exactly what he was doing. Over her sobs, he asked the speaker what the speech was to have been about, and through her sobs she squeaked out a reply. "Sounds interesting," he replied. "What were some of your main points going to be?" Again, she answered, regaining a bit of her composure. He replied, sincerely, "I'd like to know more about that; could you explain it to me?" So she began explaining; hesitantly at first, for she was still distraught and embarrassed, and then gradually

more fluently. By now, the entire class realized what our
wise professor was up to.   She was giving the speech!
Granted, it wasn't exactly the way she had planned to
perform it, and it was directed toward only one audience
member in response to his prompting, but all of the elements
of a good communicative effort and a good speech were
present. When it dawned on her a few moments later that
she was not only responding to the professor's questions, but
was also giving the speech, the transformation from
panicked performer to confident communicator was
complete. Without further prompting, she finished the last
half of the speech by talking to the entire audience in a
completely natural, comfortable, informative, and friendly
way. She returned to her seat smiling and triumphant, and
from that day on she was one of the most effective speakers
in the class.

The lesson learned from that experience—learned
not only by the speaker, but by everyone in the class—is that
the delivery phase of public speaking is simply a matter of
explaining information, and that the "style" with which we
explain things to a single individual in natural
conversation is, more or less, the same style we should use
in a speech. That is to say, *if we really know what we're
talking about in a speech, then all we have to do is stand up
and tell it.* It's not quite that simple, perhaps, but it is indeed
almost that simple. In any case, the performance-oriented
notion that a speaker must closely follow a prepared script,
and must be self-conscious about every behavior the

audience sees and hears, is not only a false notion, but is also a counter-productive notion.

THE CRITERION FOR GOOD SPEECHES
(FROM A COMMUNICATION PERSPECTIVE)

So, if a good speech does not depend on "perfect" language, voice, gestures, and so forth, then what does it depend on? I hope you can by now predict the answer: *A speech is a good speech when it achieves its communication goals and objectives.* What are these goals and objectives? It depends.

For almost any speech, the primary goal should be to provide the audience with information, and to do so with enough clarity that the information is understood and retained. Almost always, the information can be organized around a very few main points or themes that the speaker especially wants the audience to understand and remember. If that is the case, then one can think of a good speech as one that is successful in getting across its main points, and can think of an ineffective speech as one that does not succeed at that goal. This attitude characterizes the "communication orientation" that is almost essential both to low speech anxiety and to successful public speaking. Very simply, speakers must realize that *above and beyond other factors, a good speech is one which achieves its COMMUNICATIVE purpose.*

Successfully imparting information is not the only goal of a speaker, of course, but it almost always should be the primary goal. Notice, for example, that even in so-called "persuasive" speeches, the primary objective must be to get the audience to *understand* one's point of view, and one's reasons for that point of view. Getting them to agree with it is, in effect, a secondary goal of persuasive speeches, because agreement cannot occur unless understanding occurs first.

Still, even in so-called "informative" speeches — which is the kind most of us are called upon to give — the *primary* goal of sharing information is not the speaker's *only* goal. A typical speaker may hope, for example, to maintain credibility, to be appreciated as a decent speaker, to score "points" of one sort or another with particular audience members, to get invited back for another speech, or to accomplish any of a number of objectives. These are often quite legitimate goals, and the "communication orientation" recognizes this. The wise approach is certainly not to deny these various goals, but rather to recognize a communication-oriented priority for them. That is to say, the way to get invited back, to maintain credibility, to be appreciated by the audience, and so forth, is for the audience to view the speech as having been valuable and worthwhile. This audience view ultimately is based more on the information that is shared than on the "performance score" for the speaker.

To put it another way, it is vital that speakers concern themselves much more with the practical, or pragmatic, objectives of their speech than with their aesthetic virtues as a speaker. A speech that gets its main points across to the audience is a good speech — *period*! If it happens to be eloquent as well, that's fine; but the speaker's focus should be on the substance rather than on the eloquence. Typically, a good speech achieves its pragmatic communicative goals with no more eloquence than the speaker exhibits in ordinary conversation.

Focusing first and foremost on the communicative objectives of the speech is vitally important. And in a discussion such as this one, that might be obvious. When it comes to an actual speech, however, this pragmatic focus does not come naturally — especially for the high-anxiety speaker who has been "conditioned" toward a performance perspective. Thus, it is often necessary to make a conscious and deliberate effort to remind yourself of the importance of the communicative focus, and to consciously reduce the priority of the performance-oriented objectives.

A particularly ironic case helps to illustrate this point. It involved a young college professor who was experiencing extreme anxiety about a talk he was to give at a professional conference. The speech was supposed to report the results of research he had conducted, and the audience was to be 100 or so other professors with interests in his general research issue. The irony was in the fact that the ultimate task in giving this speech was no different than that of the lectures he gave to his classes (of about the same size, by the way) practically every day of the week — lectures in which he never experienced anxiety. Of course, he didn't see it that way.

As it turned out, the professor acknowledged that he saw his ultimate goal as having the audience conclude that he was the one of the best researchers among those giving reports at the conference. (Notice the "contest" performance orientation.) He also assumed that this required a flawless report of flawless research, and he feared that if the research appeared imperfect then the audience would challenge him. In short, he was more concerned about whether the audience would like him as a researcher than about whether the audience would understand his research report.

Eventually, he came to realize that his ego was getting in the way. He gradually took the position that he should simply present the research along with its strengths and weaknesses (as he saw it). He should expect that some audience members might challenge him. But he should view these challenges merely as the different points of view that are expected when even the most respected researchers present their reports. By the time he gave the talk, he was no longer trying to be so perfect that no "challenges" would occur, but rather was trying to be so clear about the research and its implications that "discussion" *would* occur. In short, he finally was able to see that the best way to approach this speech was exactly the same as the approach taken in the lectures to which he was already accustomed: make the *message* clear and interesting (and leave the performance ego out of it). He reported later that the "lecture" was virtually free of anxiety. And it is easy to see why: Concentrating on getting the message across is much less anxiety-arousing than wondering how one is being "sized up" by the audience. He reported also that the talk was extremely well-received by the audience. Again, it is easy to see why: The audience appreciated learning about the work the young researcher was doing, whether they viewed it as flawless or not.

So, not only is the focus on communication goals a realistic focus in terms of reducing anxiety, it is also a realistic focus in terms of satisfying the audience. Anxious speakers must recognize this and remind themselves of it repeatedly.

It is only natural for speakers to want the audience to remember them as good speakers. But usually when audiences remember speakers fondly it is because they found value *in what the speaker said,* not so much in how it was said. As a simple example of this, when I reflect on the thousands of speeches I have heard in the classroom, those that first come to mind are the ones which provided worthwhile information. One of these was a demonstration speech by a Japanese student who distributed pairs of chopsticks to each audience member, and then explained in a very clear step-by-step fashion, how to use them properly. Now, every time I use chopsticks I remember the speaker from whom I learned how, and I suspect several others in that class do as well. But the speaker is fondly remembered not because she was dynamic (in fact, she was quite shy), and not because she was eloquent (in fact, she had some difficulty with the English language), but rather because she successfully communicated a worthwhile message.

The point is that part of the communication orientation is the speaker's sincere hope that, *after the speech, the subject of thought and conversation among the audience members*

*will be the information they heard rather than the speaker
they saw.* And notice that this approach is again quite
realistic. As audience members, what do we find ourselves
discussing after speeches at business meetings,
professional conferences, PTA meetings, civic meetings,
and so forth? Usually, we find ourselves discussing what
the speakers said. About the only time we find ourselves
criticizing the speaker, per se, is when we are frustrated by
the lack of content in the speech. Notice also, that unlike our
classmates who used to count the "uhs" in our book reports,
adult audiences are extremely forgiving of minor
"imperfections" in performance skills as long as they are
getting something out of the speech content.

To put it another way, while it is natural for speakers
to want to make a good personal impression, it is imperative
that speakers assign this goal its proper priority as
subordinate to, and *dependent* upon, the achievement of the
communicative goals. Certainly, it is fine for speakers to
hope for compliments after the speech, but it is important—
both for anxiety-reduction and for speaking effectiveness
— to properly prioritize the desired compliments. Feedback
indicating that our performance style was enjoyed and
appreciated is nice, to be sure, but it is secondary. Speakers
should regard the highest compliment to be that their
message was understood and appreciated. To put it very
simply, audiences listen to speeches to hear what speakers
have to say, rather than to judge their oratorical skills, so
speakers should arrange their own priorities accordingly.
And this is so much easier than the other way.

PREVIEWING A LOW-ANXIETY APPROACH
TO DELIVERY

In addition to reducing anxiety and satisfying the audience, there is one more benefit of the communicative perspective worth mentioning. Specifically, focusing on communicative objectives rather than on performance behaviors almost always makes for a better speech delivery. While delivery will be the specific subject of the next chapter, it is helpful to understand a few basic points within the context of the present discussion of the communication orientation. In particular, notice the irony: Delivery, the main concern of the anxiety-inducing performance orientation, actually *improves* when the preoccupation with delivery behaviors is abandoned in favor of a concern for pragmatic communication objectives!

This is because good delivery is not so much a matter of stringing together a series of "perfect" performance behaviors as it is a matter of displaying an overall delivery *attitude*. As was suggested in Chapter 1, the ideal delivery is one which has *directness*. Recall that directness is the feeling or impression by the audience members that the speaker is truly relating to them and communicating with them, rather than impersonally orating for the sake of orating. To a very large degree, directness translates as *sincerity*, and sincerity is primarily attitudinal. That is to say, directness in delivery depends to a large extent on the speaker's sincere desire to *communicate* with the audience.

In case that sounds obvious, notice what happens to directness and sincerity in most performance-oriented speeches.   Speakers concerned more about their own performance than about the audience's understanding of their message often seem to lack directness and sincerity. If the performance-oriented delivery is indeed "perfect," then the speech usually seems "phony." And if the delivery is "imperfect," the performance-oriented speaker often becomes visibly "flustered." In either case, the problem occurs because the speaker's objective is not so much to take advantage of an opportunity to share information with the audience, as it is to survive the speech experience with a decent performance.

Think about this for a moment. Have you ever given a speech in which your true underlying objective was to get it over with? If so, you can identify with a performance perspective. The performance-oriented speaker hopes to survive the speech without major mishaps, just as the Olympic gymnast hopes to get through a routine without errors. If successful, both give a sigh of relief when it is over. But wanting to survive and get it over with is hardly the attitude that makes for directness and sincerity in the delivery of speeches. In contrast, the communication-oriented speaker is concerned with *taking advantage of an opportunity to tell the audience something that is important.* And that attitude, unlike its opposite, is indeed conducive to a sincere and direct delivery.

Delivery Behaviors Should be Natural. It is a bit vague, I realize, to talk about the target of delivery in terms of an *attitude* when we are used to discussing public speaking delivery in terms of *behaviors*. I assure you that we will be discussing specific delivery behaviors in the next chapter. Previewing the theme of that discussion may help to put the present discussion in context, however. Specifically, the theme of our later discussion on delivery behaviors—gestures, facial expression, word choice, etc.—will be, "*be natural.*" Naturalness is the key to directness, and directness is the key to an effective delivery.

Think about it this way: Who are the country's very best actors and television news reporters, and what is it that makes them outstanding? No matter who you happen to select in your answer, chances are that you will agree that what makes them especially good is their directness, or apparent naturalness—the feeling that they are talking on the screen the same way they would be talking if they were in your own living room or den. Apparently, directness and ostensible naturalness represent the goal of the ideal performance. Transferring the same goals to public speaking, this gives the speaker a couple of choices: either be such a good *actor* that you can successfully *fake* naturalness and directness during your delivery performance, or forget the performance and simply *be communicatively natural and direct in the first place.* Guess which is easier!

It should be obvious that the latter choice is much easier for the typical speaker. Less obvious, perhaps, but important to recognize, is what happens when the amateur tries the first approach (faking directness): The typical performance-oriented speaker *is* artificially inhibited, and *appears* artificial and inhibited to the audience. Notice that professional actors and news anchors are inhibited by their scripts, and are in communicatively artificial contexts (since their true audience is not present). The good ones, however, are able to transcend these restrictions, as we noted a moment ago. Performance-oriented speakers, on the other hand, are in a communicatively real context (since their communicative partners are present), so that should make directness much easier.

Unfortunately, however, the performance-orientation often leads speakers to "script" their speeches in a way that is terribly inhibiting. At the extreme, some performance-oriented speakers memorize their speech word for word. In terms of effective speaking, a memorized speech is almost always fatal. First, it activates anxiety, because the speaker subconsciously recognizes the extreme consequences of forgetting what was supposedly memorized. (More on that later.) Secondly, and more to the present point, memorization severely restricts the speaker's choices, and completely strips the speaker of spontaneity. And it happens that natural gestures, facial expression, and other delivery behaviors are tied to naturally spontaneous talk. Thus, when spontaneity goes, naturalness goes; and when naturalness goes, directness goes. The "half-memorized" speech—the type which is still tightly scripted, but whose script is partly memorized and partly prompted by note cards—has very much the same effect. The only way to get a good delivery out of a scripted speech is to be such a good actor that ostensibly spontaneous delivery behaviors accompany the script. Overly-scripted speeches make it easy to "get it over with," but they make the speaker come across as artificial, phony, inhibited, and easily flustered.

The communication-oriented speaker, on the other hand, works not with a script, but rather with an outline of ideas, points, illustrations, examples, and other overall communicative objectives of various kinds. (We'll elaborate on this in Chapter 4.) The communicative *objectives* and *strategies* of the speech are very carefully planned, but the actual words used are, for the most part, quite spontaneous. The attitude is something like this: "I know my subject, I know the points I want to get across, I know the organization and strategies I've planned, so why should I script the speech? I know how to speak the language, so I'll just use my own words in trying to get my points across." For the most part, this communicative attitude takes care of concerns about particular delivery behaviors. A sincere communicative effort with a large dose of spontaneity helps to ensure that the delivery behaviors will be natural rather than phony, and that they will be less inhibited.

HOW THE COMMUNICATION PERSPECTIVE
REDUCES ANXIETY

The "bottom line" is that we already know how to communicate. We all have successful everyday conversations, both casual and serious. There is room for improvement in our everyday conversation, certainly, but we've generally mastered the basics. And except for special situations (like job interviews, asking someone special for a date, etc., which aren't truly "everyday" situations), we carry on our communication encounters without anxiety. Now, if we already know how to communicate, and a speech is primarily a communication episode, then we already know how to give a speech. And if we already know how, then there's no reason to be anxious about whether we can do it.

Think back to the classroom exercise described in Chapter 1. The speech begins with only one audience member present. As the speaker "converses" with that single individual, two or three additional audience members join the "conversation," and the remainder of the audience gradually trickles in until all are present. If all goes well, nothing about the speaker's style or delivery changes as the audience size increases from one to many. The speaker is directing the communication to more individuals, but is doing so the same way it was being done with one. As for when the "conversation" became a "speech," there is a true sense in which it *never* does. But if it does, the switch depends on the *attitude* of the speaker more than on anything else.

There are, of course, definitional differences between a "conversation" and a "speech," but let's look closely at those. I would argue that there are only two differences, as implied earlier. The first is that in a speech we usually talk longer without interruption. The other is that for a speech we spend more time planning the message. You might argue that there is a third difference in the relative sizes of the audience, but consider this: Let's say that I call someone into my office to discuss a conflict we are having, and give them a long, uninterrupted "spiel" that I spent a lot of time planning. Is that a "speech" or a "conversation?" We could argue either way, I suppose, but in many ways it is like a speech, even though there is only one audience member. The point here is similar to that of the earlier example where the speaker began with only one audience member present, and the others gradually filtered into room during the talk: It's really not the number of people present that differentiates between a converstaion and a speech.

In any case, notice that these two or three definitional differences between conversation and public speaking should not pose a threat to the speaker. First, the fact that more time goes into the preparation of a speech is clearly an advantage over conversation. When we prepare, we are following the familiar "think before you speak" adage that is helpful in virtually any communication situation. Secondly, the fact that we are less frequently interrupted as public speakers represents an advantage as well, since it means that we have more control against digressions from our communicative goals. Finally, if you insist that the size of the audience makes a difference, then notice that a larger audience is a bonus in favor of efficiency (at least from the communication perspective). With a larger audience we are able to share our ideas and information with more communication partners in one fell swoop.

So, the "big picture" in terms of reducing speech anxiety via the communication perspective is that anxiety tends to subside when a speech is viewed as more similar to normal communication than to performance. This is partly because much less anxiety is already associated with the familiar conditions of communication than with the novel requirements of performance. And if orienting toward communication goals and attitudes makes for better speeches as well, then it makes even more sense to do so.

A little earlier we contrasted methods by which speech teachers may grade speeches. In effect, these represent also the demands speakers may put upon themselves. All speakers want to do well on their speeches, but there are choices as to what it means to do well. One approach is to imagine being graded by a check-list of behaviors. The wiser approach is to imagine being graded according to a hypothetical content-oriented quiz taken by the audience. That is to say, the speaker should imagine a set of questions that would test only whether the points got across. If, after the speech, the audience can pass the quiz, then the speaker has passed the test of a good speech. I'm suggesting an imaginary questionaire that contains items on whether the audience understood key points, but contains not a single item to measure the audience reaction to the speaker's behaviors. In real life, speakers don't get a chance to actually test the audience, of course, but this imaginary examination represents the proper approach to the speaker's objectives. It suggests that the speech is a good one if the audience is made to understand certain key points — *period!* This puts the speaker's focus on taking the trouble to prepare and plan the speech so as to ensure that the speech contains clear and worthwhile messages, and this is where the speaker's focus should be. It also takes the focus off the need to devise artificial performance behaviors for the delivery of those messages.

This approach more closely matches the audience's wishes for the speech. Moreover, confidence in one's ability to successfully communicate certain messages is easier to come by (providing one has taken care with planning the content, organization, and strategies) than confidence in one's ability to score performance points. As for the fact that speeches have style as well as substance, remember that as long as substance is present, the ideal style in almost every case is that of natural direct conversation. Again, given this orientation to public speaking, you may be confident that, as far as delivery behaviors are concerned, there is nothing about giving a speech that you don't already know how to do.

THE IRRATIONAL FEARS

As we have discussed already, part of the public-speaking anxiety cycle is a psychological process in which the speaker attempts to justify the feelings that have been interpreted as fear. That is to say, the anxious speaker usually has discovered or invented certain reasons to be afraid. These reasons tend to fall into two major categories. One goes something like this: "I always do badly in certain kinds of situations (novel situations, formal situations, evaluative situations, etc.), and public speaking is that kind of situation." The other category of fears is represented by comments along these lines: "If I make such-and-such a kind of error in my speech, the audience will ridicule me," where the hypothetical error might be most any performance-oriented faux pas of public speaking.

Most often, these fears are irrational in that they do not represent the realities of public speaking. One of the positive fringe benefits of the communication orientation is that it helps put these fears into a more rational light. I have listed below the most common responses by anxious speakers to the question of exactly what their object of fear is assumed to be. And I have also provided the more rational alternative to these common responses. If you are an anxious speaker, some of the concerns listed will match your own specific "fears," and others will not. It should be helpful to read through the entire list in any case, since all of the rational alternatives—the answers to these common concerns—amplify the communication perspective.

So, what exactly are speaker's "afraid of" when they experience public-speaking anxiety, and are those "fears" legitimate? Let's take a look.

1. The audience will ridicule me if I make a mistake. Probably the most common "fear" mentioned by anxious speakers is that they will be humiliated by mistakes in their speech. When asked what kind of mistakes might cause this humiliation, typical answers include minor "errors" such as losing one's place in the speech, forgetting parts of the speech, making slips of the tongue, and so forth. Sometimes the answers include more general performance shortcomings, such as bad eye contact, poor gestures, and the like. As for whether these are rational fears, the answer lies in the question of whether mature audiences do in fact ridicule speakers for these kinds of "errors." Do they? Of course not! How do we know this? We know by examining our own behavior as *audience* members.

When you are in an audience and the speaker makes a mistake, do you ridicule the speaker? Almost certainly not, especially if you are getting something worthwhile from the speech. Think about this and see if you don't agree that almost every speech we hear as an audience member contains a few "errors," yet very rarely do we even notice, much less ridicule the speaker. And if we are this forgiving of errors by speakers we hear, then doesn't it stand to reason that your audiences will be equally forgiving of your errors?

Now, if you wanted to be a bit dogmatic about the risk of ridicule, you could argue that although it is admittedly rare for errors to result in ridicule, there nevertheless have been those rare occasions on which you have ridiculed speakers for errors. And you could argue that, as a speaker, you don't want the same to happen to you. But think about those rare instances in which errors cause ridicule, and I think you will agree that they have always been situations in which the speaker was, because of an inappropriate attitude toward the audience, practically "asking for it." Speakers who display a superiority, or "holier than thou" attitude, for example, are likely to be ridiculed for errors because they act as if they don't believe themselves capable of errors. Obviously, however, speakers with high anxiety are not likely to display that attitude, for overconfidence is not their problem. Likewise, speakers who do not seem sincere in their desire to communicate clearly with their audience also are viewed by the audience as "asking for it." But communication-oriented speakers do have a sincere desire to communicate, and if one has it, it shows.

It is extremely difficult to imagine an audience ridiculing a speaker who is engaged in a sincere effort to communicate ideas. Small errors are easily ignored in these cases, and major catastrophes are easily forgiven.

Let me relate a case in point. Several years ago, I attended a conference at which one of the speakers—a respected colleague—fainted during his speech. About three minutes into the speech, he gradually slowed down and then simply collapsed behind the podium. After a few minutes during which first aid of some sort was administered, he struggled to his feet, explained that he had had problems with hypoglycemia, and continued his speech. As unforseen problems in speeches go, this certainly was a big one. When anxious speakers say that they fear ridicule if something goes wrong with their speech, it would be difficult to imagine anything "going wrong" worse than fainting. So, take a guess at the audience reaction when the speaker fainted. Ridicule? Of course not. The audience was worried, concerned, and sympathetic. And what was the audience reaction long after the incident? Again, not ridicule, but rather admiration for the perserverence, and appreciation for the information.

In short, the fear that errors cause audience ridicule or speaker humiliation is an irrational fear. Unlike our grade-school classmates, mature audiences do not ridicule speakers for errors as long as the speaker is sincerely making an effort to communicate worthwhile information.

2. I'm going to make a fool of myself. When anxious speakers say that they fear making "fools of themselves," I like to ask them just what sort of events would be required in order for that to happen. In other words, what would it take to make a total fool of yourself in a speech? When we stop and think about it, we realize that making a total fool of oneself in a speech is in fact very difficult to do. The evidence again comes from our own experience as audience members. We've all heard speeches that we didn't like, but how many times have we seen anyone suffer a complete "loss of face" as a result of giving a speech? Almost never. Now, if you can think of one or two instances where it did happen, reflect back on whether those speakers seemed to be trying more to impress you with themselves, or trying more to communicate ideas about their speech subject. I think you will agree that sincerely communicative speakers can hardly make fools of themselves, even if the speech is not particularly outstanding.

As I reflect back on the many speeches I have heard, I can think of only two in which the speakers were on the one hand sincerely communicative and on the other hand made total fools of themselves. (By that I mean that the audience not only failed to enjoy the speech, but completely lost respect for the speakers as individuals.) Both were cases in which the speaker was highly insulting and offensive to significant portions of the audience, and cases in which this was obvious to everyone except the speaker. One involved gross insensitivities to racial stereotyping, and the other concerned gross insensitivities to certain common religious beliefs. As you might guess, both were by speakers with very low speech anxiety who got up and started spouting off without much forethought. It is difficult to imagine an anxious speaker offending the audience in this manner, because anxious speakers are inherently concerned with the audience response.

In short, speakers who are concerned about making fools of themselves must realize that the odds of that happening are infinitesimally small to begin with, and smaller still when a sincere communicative effort is attempted. Whatever the outcome of our speech, it's not likely to be that we look foolish.

3. I'm afraid that I won't be perfect. The fear that the speech will be less than perfect is a variation of the two fears already mentioned, and is a direct by-product of the performance orientation we have discussed at length. By now, you can probably see that the concern for perfection is somewhat irrational. I doubt that any of us has ever heard a perfect speech, if "perfect" means what anxious speakers usually mean when they discuss this fear; that is, a speech with no perceptible mistakes. Certainly, even the best speeches of our most respected speakers turn out to be full of

mistakes when we play back recordings and actually look
for errors. (Try this with a VCR sometime if you don't
believe it.) The point is not that these speeches aren't so
great after all, since they contain mistakes. Rather, the
point is that good speeches are good speeches despite their
"mistakes."

It is interesting to note, by the way, that professional
speakers who give the same speech so often that they can "do
it in their sleep" actually *plan* certain ostensible mistakes
just so that the speech will *not* be perfect. The errors are
designed to make the audience see them as a "real person."
I'm not advising that, of course. The point is simply that in
an otherwise effective speech, minor mistakes do not
seriously detract, so they should not be feared. Just as in
normal conversation, some mistakes are so trivial that we
let them go unacknowledged, and the others we catch,
correct, and forget.

**4. I'm afraid because for me public speaking is an
unfamiliar situation.** It is common for speakers to blame
their anxiety on the novelty or unfamiliarity of the public
speaking situation. The clichéd speech introduction,
"unaccustomed as I am to public speaking . . .," is in some
ways an attempt to gain audience sympathy for having to
sink or swim in what the performance orientation sees as
the mysterious unknown territory of public speaking. If the
novelty of the situation is indeed responsible for the fear,
then the solution should be a simple matter of recognizing
that *while we may not be used to performing, we are indeed*

used to communicating. That is to say, if we view the speech as a performance, then probably it is indeed a relatively unfamiliar situation. But if we view a speech as a communication event, and if we agree, as discussed above, that it need not be terribly different from ordinary conversation, then the novelty explanation for the fear can be countered. We may be unaccustomed to performing, but we are quite accustomed to communicating and sharing our information and views with listeners. We do it everyday.

5. I get uncomfortable when I have to be formal. Some speakers claim that their anxiety comes not so much from a concern about making a few incidental mistakes, as from not knowing how to act in the more general sense. Their feeling is that speakers need to be formal, that formality implies a certain "air" or "bearing," and that this requires an overall mode of behavior with which they are unfamiliar or uncomfortable. The answer for these speakers has to do with the matter of just *how* formal a public speaker needs to be.

Speakers who are too *informal* tend to lose the respect of the audience, while speakers who are too *formal* can appear stuffy. As for the earlier advice to behave in speeches very much as in conversation, most of us can easily imagine that approach leading to an excess of informality. After all, surely we shouldn't talk to a speech audience the same way we talk during our more crude, or raunchy, or euphoric, or cathartic moments. So, how can we be natural and conversational during a speech without appearing too informal to the audience?

The formula for formality in public speaking has to do with respect for the audience and respect for the situation. When we discuss parallels between public speaking and conversation, think in terms of *serious* conversation. The implication is that public speaking attitudes and behaviors should not be considered to parallel those of any and all everyday conversation. Rather, public speaking should parallel the attitudes and behaviors of more serious conversations in which we recognize and respect the importance and the challenge of the communicative effort —that is, conversations in which we are truly "getting down to business" about something.

But there is another condition we should add at this point, especially for those concerned with formality. Namely, our public-speaking behaviors should parallel serious conversations with persons of whom we are *respectful*. Imagine having a conversation with someone you know well, *respect* highly, and converse with easily. This may be a minister, grandfather, former teacher, or whomever. Chances are, the level of "formality" your behaviors exhibit in such a conversation is about the same level of formality you would need to exhibit in a speech.

In other words, if you are anxious because of the presumed need for formality in a speech, realize that the key to a proper "air" or "bearing" for a speaker is not so much a matter of formality as it is a matter of sincerity and simple respect. We may "be ourselves" in speaking situations, but we should try to be ourselves at our best, because the audience deserves that respect, and because respect tends to be reciprocal—you respect them and they respect you. That means that we do not have to be formal in some way that is unfamiliar to us or awkward for us. Rather, we may simply act as we already know how to act when we are respectful of our listeners.

6. **I feel conspicuous being evaluated, and/or being scrutinized by the audience.** Earlier in the book I mentioned one of the most common "fears" listed by anxious public speakers in the classroom. Students often identify the object of their fear to be the impending grade, and it is easy to prove this wrong: When the instructor offers to allow the speech to be ungraded, the anxiety does not disappear. When this paradox is examined, the conclusion usually is that the anxiety remains because the speaker imagines that there will still be a mental evaluation—by the instructor and by the fellow students—even if no grade is officially recorded. The idea that you are being evaluated implies that you are being scrutinized by the audience. Nobody likes being under a microscope, so it is easy to see how anxiety would follow.

We have indirectly discussed the reply to this fear already. "Real world" audiences do not put our speech behaviors under a microscope. Instead, they focus on the message. Thus, if the speaker has taken care to prepare meaningful points of information, and successfully concentrates the effort on communicating the corresponding messages, then there is no need to be concerned about audience scrutiny. The audience attention will be on what is being said.

It is natural to feel a bit conspicuous, I suppose, when we think of "all those eyes" focused on us. But the proper attitude about this, I think, comes with the pragmatic communication perspective. Many of us are likely to say that we don't like feeling overly conspicuous, and some will say that we don't like being the center of attention. Even the most introverted of us, however, will acknowledge that when we have something important to say to someone, we like for them to listen. And that is precisely the way to view what is going on during a speech.

We've all had the experience of being caught off guard with a group's attention focused on us, and most of us find those situations uncomfortable, granted. But a speech isn't like that. A speech is a situation in which we have some important thoughts we want to share. And we are not caught off-guard, because we are prepared to share those thoughts. In these situations, we *do* want attention, at least in the sense that we want our ideas to be heard. The anxious speaker who believes the fear to be based on audience attention should ask whether it would be better to face an audience that *wasn't* paying attention! (And if facing an inattentive audience does sound attractive, then the communication orientation is missing!)

7. I'm afraid that the audience will be able to detect my anxiety. Some speakers are embarrassed by their anxiety, and the fear of displaying it to the audience compounds the problem. Usually this fear operates during the speech itself, perhaps especially in the introduction. The speaker imagines that the audience perceives one or more signs of anxiety, the resulting embarrassment triggers another sign, and so on, causing a "snowball" effect. Using a slightly exaggerated example, the speaker's thoughts go something like this: "Oh, my gosh, they can tell that my voice is quivering . . . *now* they can tell that my hands are shaking . . . *now* they can tell that my knees are shaking . . . *now* they can tell that I've fainted!"

In a few cases, thoughts of displaying anxiety to the audience dominate the speaker far in advance of the speech itself, and for some speakers the primary fear object is expressed as, "I'm afraid that they will know I'm nervous." Typically, this fear is expressed by speakers who assume that public-speaking anxiety contradicts a particular reputation or image the audience has of them. I recall, for example, one high-anxiety speaker who said that he had a reputation for being "afraid of nothing." I recall another who said that he had a reputation as an excellent speaker, and yet another who had a reputation as an expert on general anxiety! It is easy to see how these individuals would be embarrassed for the audience to know of their stage fright. And indeed, the fear of being found out was overwhelming in these cases.

It happens, however, that there is very good news for those whose fear is that the audience will see their anxiety. Specifically, audiences simply are very poor judges of the amount of anxiety a speaker is experiencing. Several scientific studies have produced this conclusion. In some of these studies, audiences were listening "naturally," without necessarily paying attention to anxiety, and were then asked to gauge the anxiety of the speakers they had heard. In these cases, audiences far *under*estimated the speakers' actual anxiety levels. In other experiments, audiences have been instructed in advance to pay attention to speakers' anxiety levels. In these cases it again turns out that audiences are terribly inaccurate in judging a speaker's anxiety.

A nice little demonstration of the same point takes place in some speech classes. After students deliver one of their first speeches, the instructor asks the audience, "How many of the speakers appeared to you to be nervous?" The answer usually is zero, or close to zero. But when the instructor asks, "How many of those who spoke today experienced stage fright during the speech?" virtually every speaker's hand goes up. Everybody had it; nobody showed it!

It happens that anxiety manifestations which are very obvious to speakers themselves are in fact much more covert than speakers assume. The "quivering voice," for example, is something that speakers <u>feel</u> more than <u>hear</u>. While the trembling of the laryngeal muscles is obvious to the speaker, the actual acoustic consequences are usually much too subtle for the audience to perceive. Generally, the same is true for other anxiety manifestations, as well. They are much more obvious to the speaker than to the audience.

Granted, a few speakers manifest their anxiety almost voluntarily, as when speakers say, "You'll have to excuse my nervousness," or hold a loose sheet of paper in trembling hands instead of laying it on the podium, or wear open collars or low-cut blouses when their neck is turning red from the anxiety. These are exceptional cases, however. As a rule, the speaker's belief that the audience can detect the anxiety simply is not true.

You don't have to take my word for it, or that of the several studies supporting the claim. You can prove the point for yourself, and I advise doing so if you are especially concerned with your anxiety being detected. It can be extremely enlightening and comforting to ask an audience member, after your speech, whether your nervousness showed. (Of course, you have to pick an audience member whom you know well enough both to confess the anxiety and to trust the feedback.) Hearing a trusted audience member tell you that the anxiety didn't show (and I can almost assure you that this will happen) can be most helpful in relieving the fear of being perceived as an anxious speaker.

8.   I'm afraid because I never give good speeches. Some anxious speakers reply, when asked to specify why they are afraid, "I just can't give a speech," "I always panic," "I never give good speeches," and the like. The temptation is to counter these responses with a motivational mini-sermon on defeatist attitudes, reminiscent of stories like "The Little Engine that Could." But there is an easier approach. Invariably, speakers who are convinced that they have always failed in the past turn out to be speakers who have always taken a performance approach to their speeches.

Thus, there are two good answers to those whose fear is based on variations of the claims "I know I can't do it because I've always failed before." One reply is, "You wouldn't know because you've never tried it," and the other is, "You do it all the time."

Although these replies may appear contradictory, I think you can see that they are not. The first—you've never tried it—means that you can't claim to have always failed at public speaking when all of your past experience has been with performing. Unless you've failed at a true pragmatic communicative effort, you can't claim that you've failed at speaking. That is to say, from a communication perspective those earlier efforts weren't speeches, they were performances. So before saying that you can't do it, see what happens when you give your first real (communication oriented) speech.

The second reply—"you do it all the time"—means that, from a communication perspective, we constantly do what is required of a speech via the serious communication efforts in our everyday lives. Putting these two answers together, the point is that it is unrealistic to base one's anxiety upon past experiences with performance-oriented speeches. The communication orientation provides an approach that is very different than that of the earlier speeches, but one with which we are in fact quite familiar, and generally successful, in our everyday lives.

9. I'm afraid that: I won't make sense . . . or . . . someone will disagree with me . . . or . . . it won't turn out the way I planned . . . etc. It is rare, but occasionally an anxious speaker's stated fear object has to do with uncertainty about the audience response to the speech message.   As speech-anxiety fears go, these are encouraging because they at least manifest a communication orientation to the speech. In a sense, these are the only "legitimate" concerns a speaker should have. Of course, if the concern is exaggerated into fear, then there are problems.

Once a speaker wholeheartedly adopts a pragmatic and communicative approach to speaking, much more than half the anxiety battle is won. Still, it is possible to put unreasonable demands on oneself even within the communication perspective. And unreasonable demands can foster anxiety because of a subconscious realization that the unreasonable demands are not likely to be satisfied. It is unreasonable, for example, to expect that a speech intended to persuade will dramatically change the attitude of every audience member holding the opposing point of view. It is not unreasonable, however, to expect that the same speech can at least make clear the speaker's point of view, and thereby lead to attitude shifts in a significant portion of the audience. Likewise, it is unrealistic to expect, in an informative speech, that every single audience member will retain 100% of the information provided; but it is reasonable to expect that the speaker's few main points will reach a significant portion of the audience.

As for what speakers can do to help ensure that realistic objectives of the speech will be satisfied, this is the subject of subsequent chapters, especially the one on speech content. The secret to eliminating the kinds of fears we are discussing now — exaggerated concern over whether the speech will achieve its communicative purpose — is found in the preparation that precedes the speech. As we will see, it is easy — with adequate preparation — to be very confident that one's speech will have its intended effect on a significant portion of the audience.

YOU MAY WANT TO REREAD THIS CHAPTER LATER

Each chapter of this book is geared to a specific dimension of an overall program to substantially reduce and control public speaking anxiety, and different speakers may find different chapters most valuable. For most high-anxiety speakers, however, the principles explained in this chapter will be the primary key.

For some readers, the principles discussed so far will have been readily accepted. For other readers, these principles, while hopefully easy to accept logically, may be more difficult to incorporate into standard practice. That is to say, for some readers, the replacement of a performance orientation with the communication orientation will be total and complete at this point, and for other readers the conversion may not yet be complete.

I strongly encourage you to return to this chapter from time to time, until the communication orientation and all of its facets and implications have become your standard way of viewing public speaking. As I said at the outset, my objective in this chapter has been to persuade you to a new way of thinking about your speeches. Ideally, you are persuaded already. If not, I hope you are persuaded at least to the point of accepting the communication-orientation principles as valid, though perhaps "easier said than done." The subsequent chapters will help to show what is involved in putting the communication orientation into practice. That should help toward understanding that the principles are almost as easily done as said.

Nevertheless, the primary thrust of the communication orientation is found not in a set of behaviors and actions, but rather in a set of speaker attitudes — both the more basic and the more subtle attitudes discussed in this chapter. If these attitudes have not yet become standard to your view of public speaking, it should be helpful to reread this chapter after reading the next few. You might wish also to reread it prior to giving your next few speeches. Once the attitudes and implications of the communication orientation become your natural, unforced, and automatic view of public speaking, the major part of the battle against anxiety will be won, and the path toward effective public speaking will be paved.

CHAPTER 4

SPEECH DELIVERY—A COMFORTABLE
AND EFFECTIVE APPROACH

In Chapter 2, I mentioned a scientific study which proved the effectiveness of this book for reducing speech anxiety. You may recall that the study obtained very impressive results using only the first three chapters. Since you've already read the first three chapters, it is quite likely that your own anxiety has already been reduced substantially. In fact, it is reasonable to expect that if you were going to give a speech, say, a week or so from now, you would—on the basis of what you've read so far—experience much less anxiety than ever before.

So you might be wondering, if the first three chapters have been proven to reduce stage fright, why do we need the remaining chapters? The next two chapters give tips on preparing and delivering your speeches. Granted, you may not need any tips. After all, you probably already have the basic idea—plan and organize your content so that it will be worthwhile and clear, then talk about it to the audience the way you usually talk in serious conversations. If you feel ready, go for it! But, in the interest of rounding out a productive journey toward reduced anxiety and improved speeches, you might be interested in ways to facilitate planning the content, and ways to facilitate talking naturally with the audience.

It may seem ironic to include a chapter on delivery. After all, a main assumption of the communication orientation is that you already have the appropriate style and behavioral skills for delivering a speech, since they are the same style and behaviors you use in everyday conversation. And essentially, that is true. Over and over, this chapter is going to advise, "be natural." But just as your earlier performance orientation came from misconceptions you learned elsewhere, there are some persistent myths and misconceptions about speech delivery that should be dispelled if you've heard them before. Also, there are specific approaches to delivery, which if considered in advance, can make the communication orientation easier to remember and put into practice. And there are delivery tips that serve both to reduce anxiety and to make speeches more effective.

In this chapter we will look at the communication-orientation approach to each of several aspects of delivery, and in each case the advice will be consistent with contemporary teaching. In particular, we will discuss overall style, gestures, speech rate, eye contact, and the use of notes versus reading or memorizing.

GENERAL STYLE—DIRECTNESS

An old song includes the lyrics, "It ain't what you say, it's the way that you say it." Of course, the song was referring to romance, not speeches. In speeches, it matters very much what you say *and* how you say it. But the difficult part is "what you say"—planning and organizing the main points, examples, illustrations, and so forth. "How you say it," with respect to such things as manner, delivery, and so forth, is important also. But it is fairly easy.

As you may recall from the preceding chapters, the most important aspect of your overall delivery is *directness*. Again, directness is the general feeling that the speaker is genuinely talking *with* the audience, rather than talking *at* the audience, or orating in some sort of oblivious monologue. And as you can guess by now, the advice for how to be direct is simply, *be natural* —talk the same way that you would in a conversation with an acquaintance you respect.

This assumes that the "what you say" has been carefully planned, but that the "how you say it" is mostly spontaneous. In other words, your content should be well organized and well thought out, but it should not be memorized, written out to be read, or otherwise scripted. (This is because memorized speeches and scripted speeches almost always sound artificial, non-natural, and non-direct. More on this later.) Rather, the assumption is that you will use very brief notes. The notes will be to remind yourself of *what* you are going to talk about, and in what order. But as for *how* to say it—what words to use, what gestures, facial expression, and so forth—you should let natural spontaneity take care of that, just as it does in natural conversation.

It is very important to recognize that I am not suggesting that you merely *act* natural, but that you truly *be* natural. Here is a real-life example of what I mean: A couple of years ago a friend took a new job as a public-relations representative. Her duties included going to various schools and giving one of a dozen or so one-hour speeches that her new company had prepared for its public-relations team. For weeks, she had labored and fretted over just two of these speeches. Her husband, a speech instructor, had been correctly advising her all along not to memorize the speeches, but rather to focus on the main points and express them in her own words. As the deadline for her first speech approached, she became more frantic. He finally realized that she didn't understand what he was advising, and offered to demonstrate what he meant. He took one of the scripts, spent a while reading it over a few times, and made a brief outline. After about an hour, he came back to his wife and gave the speech very effectively from very sketchy notes. She was simultaneously amazed and frustrated that he managed to master in an hour what she had spent several weeks working on so laboriously. Her reaction was, "That was fantastic! Why can't *I* do that?" His reply: "You *can*. Take *my outline* and explain each of the points *in your own words*." He gave her his sketchy outline, she tried it, and it worked. She did likewise when the speeches were "for real," and it worked every time. By the way, she soon became the "model" speaker used to train new members of the firm's public-relations team.

The point of this story in our present context is that while this speaker had been advised from the beginning not to memorize the speeches and just to use her own words, she had been resistant to the idea of being spontaneous. She had been trying to use her own words, she explained later, but had been trying to get those words "down pat" before giving the speech. She was trying to ignore the original script, granted, but she was trying to replace it with another script. The demonstration by the husband, and her subsequent approach, makes the point I'm trying to make here: When I advise that you be natural and spontaneous, I am advising that once you are comfortable with your content — your knowledge of it, organization of it, etc. — that you be *truly* spontaneous.

This doesn't mean that you should "wing it" completely. (We'll discuss preparation, practicing, and so forth later.) But it means that you need to be truly talking naturally and spontaneously with the audience.

Let me give one more example to emphasize this point. In my public-speaking classes we do a very effective exercise to focus on delivery. I call it the "workout" session, because it is designed to "work out" delivery problems. The speakers come to class prepared to give their speeches, and the instructor announces that the rules have been changed. Today the instructor will interrupt the speaker, at will, to fine-tune any delivery problems. With the instructor, the speakers work on one or two delivery problems until they are solved. All of this is done within the first couple of minutes of the speech. When the delivery problems are solved, the speaker sits down and the next speaker comes up. (Everyone gives their speech "for real" during the next class period.)

By far the most common "delivery problem" targeted in this exercise is simple lack of directness. (Probably this is because the "workout" session is always at the beginning of the term, before the communication orientation has been introduced.) The memorized, read, or semi-memorized speech sticks out like a sore thumb, usually right from the introduction. To point out (and "work out") the problem, the instructor simply interrupts the speaker and asks questions about the forthcoming content. "So you're going to tell us about such-and-such; what angle are you going to take? How did you get interested in that? What are some of your main points going to be?" Etc. The object, of course, is to get the speaker talking in a natural spontaneous style. Most speakers break into their natural mode immediately. Invariably, though, some resist, trying instead to answer the questions by inserting some of the "pat" material planned for later in the speech. This usually develops into a good-natured tug-of-war, with the instructor prompting the speaker toward spontaneity, and the speaker trying to hang on to the precious preplanned words. Every time, though, when the speaker finally gives up the pat speech and starts talking more spontaneously—first with the instructor, then with the audience—several things happen: The audience reports that the speaker seems more direct and easier to listen to; the speaker reports that it is easier and more comfortable talking with the audience than reciting the pat material; and the speaker also reports that the experience becomes much more relaxed.

I can't emphasize enough that directness requires a fair amount of true spontaneity. Trying to merely *act* direct while confining oneself to a pat script defeats the purpose. One needs to be truly conversational, truly direct, truly spontaneous, truly natural. The following sections discuss a few specifics.

GESTURES---Be Natural

As kids, my friends and I used to annoy one another with a little gimmick. While one of us would be talking, the others would—for no good reason—stare at his hands. The talker invariably would become self-conscious about his gestures. Usually he would quit gesturing, find himself not knowing what to do with his hands, and in frustration eventually plead, "Stop it, you guys!" The others would snicker at having gotten his goat.

Childish, to be sure, but this little game—which, by the way, works even better on adults—demonstrates an important point about gestures: They are *supposed to be non-conscious.* That is to say, in natural conversation we use gestures every day *without thinking about them.* And when we *do* consciously think about our gestures, they become *uncomfortable* and *inhibited.*

So the best advice with respect to gestures during a speech is to not think about gestures at all. For one, they're not that important. Almost never will one's gestures "make or break" a speech. But more importantly, gestures take care of themselves when they are on spontaneous automatic pilot. In conversation, some of us gesture a little, some of us gesture a lot. But virtually no one gestures improperly. In speeches, we should turn the gestures over to our non-conscious automatic pilot—that is, just let them happen naturally. This makes for appropriate gestures, and more directness. Furthermore, it gives us one less thing to worry about during the speech.

Myths. Unfortunately, some speakers find this easier said than done. That is, some find it difficult *not* to be self-conscious about gestures during their speech. It's a safe bet that the reason these speakers are overly concerned is that they have received misguided advice about gestures at some point in their past.

Thinking back to the advice most of us have heard about gestures—what to do or not do with our hands—there are two main problems with it. The first is that we'd probably all be better off if the teachers, parents, and others who gave us advice on public speaking had left gestures out of the equation altogether. To some extent, *any* advice about gestures to the young, uninitiated speaker is bad advice. Gestures simply aren't that important to speeches in the overall scheme of things (especially if directness is present). But they make easy targets of attention by teachers, especially those with performance orientations. The consequence is that these teachers, without realizing it, are playing the children's focus-on-the-hands game that I mentioned earlier. By making comments about gestures, they misdirect speakers' attention onto their gestures. This leads to inhibited gestures, the frustration of not knowing what to do with one's hands, and so forth. It really is true, I believe, that very few speakers would consider gestures to be problematic if our childhood speech advisors hadn't blown their importance way out of proportion.

The second main problem with most advice you've probably heard about gestures is that it usually takes the form, "DON'T . . . ." When this implies, "Don't *ever* . . .," it is simply very bad advice. Some common variations are; don't put your hand(s) in your pocket, don't hold the podium, don't fold your hands in front of you, and so forth. In fact, however, there is nothing wrong with holding the podium, putting a hand in a pocket, or any of these supposedly taboo behaviors. Ideally, of course, your hands should move as they normally do. But this naturalness tends to happen as you feel more comfortable in the speech situation. If it feels comfortable to put your hands on the podium, do it. If it feels comfortable to put a hand in your pocket, do it. And so forth. Once you're doing what's comfortable for you—once you stop thinking about it—you'll probably start gesturing naturally without even realizing that you're doing it. (And if not, it's no big deal.)

So, advice to never do such-and-such with your hands can create a problematic cycle. First, the advice removes all of your options for what to do with your hands when you happen not to be gesturing. It removes the podium option, the pocket option, etc. This creates awkwardness, which focuses the speaker's attention on gestures, which in turn inhibits them. And, of course, once gestures are inhibited, where else can the hands comfortably go except to the podium, pockets, etc.? But if those options are prohibited, then the cycle repeats.

Now, you may be wondering why it is that your earlier teachers emphasized gestures so much, while contemporary advice deemphasizes them. There is a very good explanation. In the early days of public-speaking instruction, the performance orientation assumed that speakers would read or memorize their speeches. This made for very mechanical-sounding speeches. The speeches lacked directness and life. To put life into these robot-like orations, speakers were taught to artificially maximize gestures, facial expression, vocal variety, and so forth. Now, notice that this is not so necessary with a communication orientation. These days the assumption is that if the speaker is talking naturally with the audience, then the "life" that comes with *natural* speech patterns eliminates the need for artificial extra efforts. To put it another way, if you are talking in a natural, conversational manner with the audience, you could be completely captivating with *zero* gestures because of the directness that comes with the conversational vocal style. Of course, I'm not advising zero gestures; I'm advising not worrying about gestures so that they happen—whether a little or a lot— naturally.

By the way, none of this is to say that there aren't things that speakers sometimes do with their hands that they shouldn't. Certainly, speakers can distract the audience if they *constantly* click their ball-point pens, play with their hair, their necklace, their tie, etc. There is nothing wrong with occasional tugs at the tie or necklace or whatever. But if the mannerism is so constant that it actually distracts the audience, then it is problematic. The good news is that these mannerisms are rarely overdone except by speakers whose anxiety is much higher than yours probably is at this point.

So, the bottom line on gestures is to realize that they are not deserving of your conscious attention during the speech. Put them on automatic pilot, and *be natural*.

In short, if you have taken a communication orientation to the speech, you will be talking much more naturally and comfortably. And if you are talking naturally and comfortably, your gestures will take care of themselves.

SPEECH RATE—Be Natural

An aspect of delivery that is problematic more often than gestures is *speech rate*—how fast the speaker talks. I'm referring here to simple words-per-minute rate. The "problem" to avoid is that of talking too fast. (Talking too slowly is rarely a problem as long as the speaker is giving worthwhile ideas to the audience. Audiences don't fall asleep because of too much time between words, but because of too much time between interesting pieces of information.) Talking too fast is another of those good-news-bad-news situations. The bad news is that going too fast is indeed a serious problem for some speakers. If the information and words are coming too fast, the audience has difficulty following and understanding the speaker. And when the audience has difficulty understanding the speaker, it is difficult for the speaker to achieve the communicative goals of the speech. The good news is that excessive rate is usually found in speakers with two related characteristics that you probably no longer have: a) a performance orientation, and b) high speech anxiety. The reason that a performance orientation causes speakers to speed up is that with a performance orientation, getting-it-over-with is more important than communicating ideas. Speakers whose goal is to get it over with tend to rush their speeches. Those who truly want to be understood tend to speak at more intelligible rates. Similarly, high speech anxiety causes speakers to rush because this is a natural consequence of excess adrenalin. Lower anxiety reduces this tendency. So, if in your past speeches you have felt that you were rushing your rate of speech, it is very likely that the communication orientation will eliminate or reduce that tendency in your future speeches.

Still, rate can be a problem even with a communication orientation, as I will discuss in a moment. As for what is the "correct" rate, any rate is fine as long as it isn't so fast that the audience has difficulty comprehending the speaker's information and ideas. When the rate is so fast that the audience experiences "information overload," then the rate is a problem.

Information overload and comprehension difficulties can occur in either of two ways. First, these difficulties can occur because the speaker's *words* are coming too fast. This is a delivery problem, and as we discussed a moment ago, it is not as likely to occur with a communication orientation. Secondly, these difficulties can occur because the speaker's *ideas* and *information* are coming too fast. This is a *content* problem, and we will give tips to avoid it in the next chapter. But it is worth mentioning here because it is a problem that actually can be *compounded* by a *communication* orientation.

If you have been giving speeches from a performance perspective, you can probably identify with the idea of a speaker increasing the speech rate so that the ordeal will end sooner. You can probably understand that the performance-oriented speaker wishes the 30-minute speech were scheduled for 20 minutes, wishes the 20-minute speech were a 10-minute speech, and so on. From a performance perspective, the shorter the speech, the less opportunity for "mistakes" that will cost "points" on the imagined critics' mental score cards. So, performance-oriented speakers tend to rush — both to get it over with, and because of their anxiety and adrenalin.

With a communication orientation, believe it or not, you will find yourself wishing there were *more* time allotted for your speech! This is because once you approach the speech as an opportunity to share your information and ideas, and to make them clear to the audience, you will discover that in most situations you will not be allotted enough time to say all that you want to say. If only there were more time, you could give a few more examples, give additional evidence, explain your position more thoroughly, introduce additional ideas and points of information, and so forth. In other words, you are going to start finding, perhaps for the first time as a speaker, that you have *too much information* for the time allotted. You will find yourself wishing you had *more* time allotted for the speech. And you may find yourself rushing again, not because of adrenalin, not to get it over with, but to cram all that you want to say into a speech that doesn't allow enough time to say it all. If you try to include too much information for the allotted time, you may end up rushing the speech. And if this causes comprehension difficulties for the audience, then it is problematic. The solution is to plan the *content* so that the most essential information is kept for the speech, and other good potential information is, unfortunately, deleted and sacrificed.

So, rate can be a problem even with a communication orientation. The best advice is to first plan the speech content such that the speech does not require the audience to handle too much new information. Then, *be natural.* Deliver the speech using the same speech rate you normally do when you are trying to *explain something carefully* in conversation.

EYE CONTACT—Be Natural (Almost)

As with other aspects of delivery, when considering *eye contact*, it is worthwhile to notice how it operates in normal conversation. Since eye contact operates differently for the person listening than for the person speaking, let's consider these separately.

It probably isn't surprising to know that as we take turns speaking and listening in natural conversation, the listeners generally look at the one who is talking—not constantly, necessarily, but most of the time. By the same token, in public speaking the audience's eyes are on the speaker most of the time. Anxious speakers sometimes report that it is disconcerting to have "all of those eyes" focused on them during a speech. Let's compare the performance orientation and communication orientation with respect to "all those eyes."

With a performance orientation, the speaker feels that "all those eyes" are scrutinizing the performance, looking for behaviors crucial to the imagined evaluation of the speaker. When a speaker believes this, and is simultaneously uncertain about the quality of the "performance," the speaker feels uncomfortable with "all those eyes," and wishes the audience would stop looking. Nobody enjoys being scrutinized.

From a communication orientation however, "all those eyes" are doing just what they do in normal conversation—*paying attention* to what the speaker is saying. When our goal is to communicate with the audience, we *want* the audience to pay attention because we think we have something worthwhile to share. From this perspective, it is more disconcerting if the audience is *not* looking at the speaker—just as it is bothersome when conversation partners appear not to be listening. Indeed, you will notice, as you deliver relatively anxiety-free speeches with a communicative goal, that the audience members who are looking at you make you more comfortable than the few who, at any given moment, may be looking elsewhere. You probably will not particularly notice "all those eyes," but if you do you will most likely appreciate them—knowing that they indicate, as in conversation, not that you are being scrutinized but rather simply that you are being listened to.

Of course, in order to appreciate that the audience is paying attention, the speaker must truly *see* the audience. This is easy to do for the communication-oriented speaker, but can be problematic for the performance-oriented speaker. It is common for high-anxiety speakers to see the audience not as individuals but rather as a mass. And sometimes it is a blurred mass. As one of my students put it, "it's as if I'm looking at them through a fog, or through a thin curtain. All the faces sort of blur together into a big jumble."

In order to have directness in delivery—to feel that you are communicating *with* the audience, the key is to speak directly with *individual* audience members—one at a time, even if for a very short time. And in order to communicate with individual audience members, it is crucial to see through the "fog"—to *see individuals*. This is much easier to do with a communication orientation than with a performance orientation, for two reasons. First, the blurring of the audience is partly a consequence of the adrenalin that accompanies high speech anxiety, and this can be expected to subside with a communication orientation.

The second reason that it is easier to "see through the fog" with a communication orientation is one that is crucial to all of the following advice on eye contact: The performance-oriented speaker — especially if the speech is read, memorized, or heavily scripted — feels a bit silly talking to individuals, because that is not the way we usually talk with individuals. It feels phony to orate while looking directly at another person — because it *is* phony. Thus, the "fog" serves as an avoidance device for performance-oriented speakers. With a communication orientation, on the other hand, it would be uncomfortabl *not* to see the audience and not to communicate directly to individual members.

To get an idea of what I mean here, imagine yourself delivering two messages. Let's call them messages "M" (for Memorized) and "S" (for Spontaneous). For message M, imagine some passage of perhaps five sentences or more that you have memorized at some point in the past — an excerpt from literature, from a historical speech or document, etc. Imagine message S to be your own thoughts or interpretations on a similar topic, or maybe simply your explanation of what message M means. Now, imagine "delivering" both messages to a friend and "delivering" both messages to a blank wall while alone. I hope you agree that message M — the memorized passage — would feel fine delivered to a wall, but a bit silly spoken one on one to a friend. And I assume you would agree that S — your own thoughts spoken spontaneously — would feel fine delivered to a friend, but awkward delivered to a wall.

Very simply, when we are trying to communicate thoughts and ideas, whether in conversation or in speeches, we are reinforced by visual contact with our listener(s). In conversation, visual contact is sometimes sacrificed, of course, as in the case of telephone conversation. But when the opportunity for visual contact is present in conversation, the person whose turn it is to speak instinctively takes advantage of the opportunity.

Notice, however, before we get to specific eye-contact recommendations for public speakers, that speakers in conversation look directly at listeners far *less* than listeners look at speakers. Rather than looking steadily at listeners for extended periods, speakers in conversation alternate between visually "touching base" with the listener(s), and looking elsewhere for short periods— especially during pauses to think of the next word or idea. There is no expectation that the speaker in conversation will make constant eye contact with an individual listener— indeed, speakers who do so make their listeners uncomfortable. Nor is there an expectation, or need, for public speakers to make constant eye contact with the audience.

The advice for public speakers' eye contact is this: It is perfectly normal and acceptable to be looking at nobody during the various momentary pauses that come with glancing at notes, searching for the right word, and so forth. (It is also o.k. to be looking at an audience member during these pauses, of course; it doesn't matter.) But most of the time that you are *actually speaking*—the time that words are coming out of your mouth—you should be, psychologically and visually, *talking to a specific individual audience member.* Talk to, and *look at*, this individual for however long it feels comfortable (which sometimes will be several seconds, other times a tiny fraction of that), and then look at and talk to a different individual audience member. It's just like conversation, where we look at the listener for whatever period feels comfortable, and then look away. *Except* that when we look away from one individual during a speech, we simply elect another individual, then another, and so on. As long as the speaker is being direct with one individual, the rest of the audience feels the speaker to be direct with them as well.

The key is to talk with *individual* audience members, *one at a time*, rather than talking with the mass, much less with a blur or a fog. In the "workout session" exercise described earlier, for example, the instructor reifies this point by interrupting the speaker to ask "who were you talking with at the moment you were interrupted." Unacceptable answers are "the front row," "the left side of the audience," "the group of five or so over in that corner," etc. The speaker starts and stops again until the answer identifies a specific individual. In short, speakers are most direct when talking—not every single moment, necessarily, but generally—to one individual audience member, then another, then another.

Eye Contact Myths. Chances are, you've never heard eye-contact goals explained quite the way we did above. And chances are, you've heard a few "tips" on eye contact that weren't included above—probably even a few that are contradicted by the approach I am suggesting.

It is worth taking a moment to discuss a few of the more common tips on eye contact, because many of them represent bad advice. Perhaps you've heard one or more of the following:

a) Instead of looking at audience members, look over the heads of the people in the last row, or

b) Instead of looking at audience members, notice an empty seat in the audience and "look at" an imaginary audience member who is sitting there, or

c) Employ "visual aids" whether you need them or not, and look at the visual aids instead of the audience.

The problem with each of these "tips" is that they advise speakers to *avoid* contact with the audience, rather than to make contact. As we noticed earlier, avoiding contact is comfortable for performance-oriented speakers, because performance behaviors are independent of an audience. But communication-oriented speakers are trying to reach listeners. We are not trying to inform empty chairs or to persuade back walls, so it makes no sense to use them as substitutes for the audience. Certainly it's alright to momentarily look at walls, empty chairs, etc. on occasion. But if you are truly trying to get your ideas across, you will feel more comfortable if you are talking directly to individual audience members most of the time.

Here is another misguided piece of advice you may have heard: "Make sure that you have made eye contact with every audience member at least once by the time you finish the speech." If you have a small audience and a long speech, it may happen that you make eye contact with each member; but if not, it doesn't matter. Certainly, though, with a shorter speech, you simply won't have time to make meaningful eye contact with each member of a very large audience. (And you'll drive yourself crazy if you try to keep track of which members you have and have not made eye contact with.) Again, it doesn't matter. As we noticed earlier, if you talk directly with a few audience members, the others will feel that you are talking with directness for them as well. As we have seen before, the proof is found in recalling your own experiences as an audience member. Surely you have been a member of an audience where the speaker seemed to be talking directly with you and everyone else, even though there was never any direct eye contact with you in particular. The speaker was being direct with everyone, but was not necessarily making eye contact with everyone.

An Old Adage Worth Keeping. After debunking some of the eye-contact advice you may have heard in the past, let's consider one you may have heard that happens to be good advice: "Pick out a few 'friendly faces' in the audience, and start out talking to those individuals (adding more 'friendly faces' as you go along)." Essentially, this says the same as we were saying a few paragraphs ago regarding talking to one individual, then another, then another. But the "friendly faces" advice is helpful in making the selection of individual target receivers intentional and non-random. It also makes the speaker proactive in "seeing through the fog." When you begin to see *individuals* in the audience, certain people will indeed appear to be especially attentive, receptive, "friendly," etc. It is very easy for speakers to spot these individuals, and of course it is natural to make these individuals your target receivers. Talk to *one* of these persons for however long it is comfortable (usually a few seconds) then another, then another, going back to particular individuals as you wish. And in the process of going from one individual to another, you will notice more and more "friendly faces"—attentive and receptive audience members who are ideal targets for relaxed communication.

There is something you can do to make seeing and talking with individuals especially easy to do. If possible, it is very much worthwhile to arrive a bit early at the place your speech is to be given, introduce yourself to one or two of the audience members who arrive early, and enjoy a short casual conversation with them about whatever comes up— serious or trivial. Psychologically, this serves as a useful reminder that the audience consists of normal individual human beings, rather than some sort of impersonal mob. It also provides "friendly faces." You will almost certainly find your attention drawn to these individuals as you begin your speech, and their familiarity will help you to "see through the fog." Moreover, it will be easier to adopt a natural and direct style when you have already had a casual conversation with one or more audience members. And chatting with a few audience members before the speech also helps in "taking the edge off" whatever mild anxiety you may feel in anticipation of the speech. For all of these reasons, you should make a practice of chatting with a few audience members in advance when it is possible to do so.

SPEECH STYLE—Be Natural

The *most* important ingredient for directness in delivery is not gestures, eye contact, speech rate, or any other delivery behavior that your earlier coaching is likely to have focused on. The most important ingredient is speech style—vocal inflections, pauses, vocal "punctuation," vocal indicators of involvement, and so forth. And the objective is to talk to the audience the way that you and other people naturally talk. If you memorize the speech, you are not likely to be direct because you won't sound natural. And if you read the speech, you almost certainly will not be direct, again because you won't sound natural.

Just as you can detect when a speech sounds read or memorized, so can others—including your audiences. And just as you would much prefer being talked to than being read to or orated to, the same is true for your audiences.

As I suggested early in the book, if we don't want to *sound* like the speech is read or memorized, we have three choices: a) Read the speech, but be such a good actor that it doesn't *sound* read; b) Memorize the speech, but be such a good actor that it doesn't *sound* memorized; or c) Don't read or memorize the speech. By far, the easiest and most effective of these choices, almost always, is *don't read or memorize the speech.*

The preferred alternative is to speak from *very brief, sketchy NOTES*. The notes are to remind you of what points you are going to make, how you will exemplify them, illustrate them, amplify them, as so forth — and to remind you of the order in which you wish to present these various points and subpoints — but NOT to give you (or even remind you of) actual preplanned words you will speak when you present your points. The word choices should happen fairly spontaneously during the speech.

When I first suggest this in one-on-one speech-anxiety consultations, it is sometimes a bit unnerving to prospective speakers. The reaction sometimes goes like this: "I've been understanding the communication orientation, and have started becoming comfortable about the idea of giving speeches; but now you're telling me to stand in front of an audience and ad lib my speech, and the thought of doing that makes me nervous all over again." It is completely understandable, even predictable, that a speaker would be anxious about completely improvising or ad libbing a speech. But that is *not* what I am suggesting.

There is a happy medium between scripting a speech so that the words are planned in advance (as with read or memorized speeches), and completely making up the speech on the spot. The idea is to prepare and organize the speech so that you are comfortable with the details you have decided to talk *about*, but to give yourself considerable latitude with respect to the exact words you will use during the actual speech. For example, some experienced speakers find that in the course of organizing and planning the speech content, they have mentally "said it to themselves" enough that they feel comfortable giving the speech with no advance practice whatsoever. But they have said it to themselves in various different ways so that they are not bound to a script. Most speakers, however, will want to practice the speech after the content has been selected and organized. And that is fine.

So how do you on the one hand practice enough to be confident that you are ready, and on the other hand allow for spontaneity during the speech? After all, if you practice too much, won't the speech become memorized? The answer— and this is crucial to maintaining directness—is to practice in such a way that you do not become psychologically committed to one "best" choice of words for the speech. Obviously there will be a few names, technical terms, and perhaps a few "gems" or other short phrases where one particular choice of words is favored. And some communication-oriented speakers like to script one or two opening and closing sentences. But for the very large majority of the speech, the idea is to avoid getting locked into particular word choices in advance.

As for how to practice while maintaining spontaneity, there are several approaches. One is to practice only once or twice so that there is virtually no way that the speech can be committed to memory. By the way, we're assuming that you are practicing from brief notes; hardly ever is there a need to write out a speech in advance (unless the press needs a copy). Another approach is to practice several times, but never aloud. By imagining several ways to say the same things, mulling over various options in your head, versatility and spontaneity are promoted. A variation of this approach is to practice aloud several times, but make a conscious effort to say things *differently* each time you practice. Another approach is to "practice" once or twice with a friend whom you have asked not so much to "listen to my speech" as to "let me tell you about something." There are other variations, of course, and each speaker should do what seems most likely to be effective in providing confidence while allowing spontaneity. The main advice I can give is that if, while practicing, you begin to realize that either a) you are trying to script the speech by locking into particular word choices, or b) without trying to script the speech you are finding yourself saying it the same way each time; then you need to stop practicing, or change your method of practicing. If you do not allow for at least a moderate amount of spontaneity with respect to word choice, you are almost certain to sacrifice directness.

One more time, notice that you already have the facility and the inclination to do what is being suggested here. Suppose, for example, that tomorrow you read a particularly interesting newspaper or magazine article, and over the next few days you tell several friends about it. You will no doubt give roughly the same information each time, and probably will present the same points and subpoints in roughly the same order each time. But you will use different words each time, and these will be the words that come to mind automatically when you are trying to get the information across to your friends. And, of course, you will have naturalness and directness each time, because your spontaneous speech will contain natural inflections and subtleties. But now, just for the sake of contrast, imagine a different situation: You read another article a week later and decide for some reason to rehearse the way you will report it to your friends. Suppose that you rehearse it so much that, knowingly or unknowingly, you have committed yourself to the words you believe should be used when you see your friends. What's going to happen when you try to tell about this article? We can imagine all sorts of outcomes, none of them very pleasant. You might decide not to tell your friends about the article at all, for fear that you won't "get it exactly right." (Remember the other reason for not memorizing is that it carries with it the fear—and the real possibility—of forgetting and becoming lost.) Or, you might go ahead and recite your preferred version perfectly, but you would sound very strange and artificial to you conversation partner in doing so. Or you might begin "perfectly" and then become anxious, frustrated, and lost when you make your first few "mistakes." The best thing that could happen, of course, would be that you begin your recitation, realize how terribly artificial it feels and sounds, and decide on the spot to abort the recitation in favor of telling what you want to say in your own spontaneous words, just as you did with the other story the week before. (Thus, it would have been better to have not over-rehearsed in the first place!)

Do realize, of course, that the main point here is not to prescribe a certain way of practicing or facilitating spontaneity. Different speakers prepare different ways, practice different ways, and achieve spontaneity in different ways. You should do what seems most comfortable to you. Whatever you think is a good way for you to be comfortably *natural* in your delivery, do it.

A CAVEAT

I began this chapter by noting that most readers will have lost a great deal of their public-speaking anxiety after reading the first three chapters of this book, and that there is irony in including a chapter in delivery. Part of the irony is that speech delivery is mostly a matter of talking the same way you do every day, so it seems a bit peculiar to present a chapter about what you already know how to do. But another part of the irony is that focusing on delivery — even if the advice generally is to be natural — hints of a performance orientation, which is just what we have been trying to avoid.

Realize that this chapter on delivery — while perhaps implying that there are "best" kinds of gestures, eye contact, vocal style, and so forth — should not deflect your communication orientation. It is *still* the case that what matters in determining whether your speeches are good speeches is whether you get across to the audience the ideas you want to get across. And you already know that you can do this, because you do it everyday with your conversation-partner audiences.

The delivery suggestions of this chapter should be viewed not as requirements for good speeches, but rather as approaches to delivery that *first* help with relaxation, and *secondly* happen to improve the speech itself. Think of these delivery suggestions as targets worth aiming for. As you progress toward any of these targets, you should notice that your anxiety about public-speaking decreases, and that most of the other targets become considerably closer. You may not hit all targets on your next speech, but with a communication orientation you are virtually certain to be much closer than you were on your last one. And after perhaps three or four speeches with these delivery suggestions in mind, all of the bullseyes will probably be there.

In the meantime, know that you can achieve your communicative objectives—that is, you can give an excellent speech—even if you don't completely "see through the fog," even if you still can't let your gestures go completely on automatic pilot, even if you're not quite ready to try more than a little bit of spontaneity, and so forth. Again, we have been focusing on these delivery ingredients not because every speech must have them in order to be successful, but rather because you will feel more and more relaxed as you begin to experience them. These are a few secondary targets of low-anxiety public speaking. The main target for effective public speaking is still simply that of getting your information across to the audience.

CHAPTER 5

KEY POINTS REGARDING SPEECH CONTENT

The theme throughout our discussion has been that the most important criterion in public speaking is that of achieving the communicative goal—getting across to the audience whatever information the speech is intended to provide. We have seen that there is very little that the speaker need worry about *during* the speech. Of course, this assumes that the content has been thoughtfully planned *before* the speech. This chapter is designed to provide a few general strategies to help with the speech content. Don't take its brevity to imply that planning your content is simple or unimportant, for certainly neither is the case.

Preparing the speech content is difficult, time consuming, and absolutely critical to the success of the speech. Indeed, standard text books on public speaking typically spend several lengthy chapters on speech content —how to research the speech, how to perform each of the various organizational and outlining strategies available, and so forth. These more lengthy treatments can be valuable in detailing specific approaches which may vary from one kind of speech to the next. The approach we will take here, however, will be to discuss more general content concerns that tend to apply to all speeches. For

communication-oriented speakers, these general
reminders and pointers usually suffice.

ANALYZING THE COMMUNICATION OBJECTIVES

We have been saying all along that a speech succeeds
to the extent that it achieves its communicative purpose. It
makes sense, then, that the first step is to decide exactly what
the communicative purpose is to be.

Most speeches can be identified as fitting one or two
standard categories with respect to their general, overall,
purpose. The most common of these is the speech *to inform*.
Most of the speeches we give in connection with our jobs and
professions, for example, are designed primarily to give
information of one kind or another to colleagues, associates,
supervisors, customers, and so forth. Obviously, the overall
objective of informative speeches is to provide the audience
with information they do not yet have, and information that
will be worthwhile for them to have.

The next most common general speech objective is *to
persuade*. Persuasive speeches are designed to reinforce or
to change particular audience beliefs, attitudes, or
behaviors. Typical campaign speeches and sales-oriented
speeches are familiar examples.

Informative and persuasive speeches constitute the
very large majority of speeches you will ever deliver, but
there are a few additional miscellaneous categories. There
are speeches to *entertain*, speeches for *ceremony*, speeches to
arouse the audience, speeches to *introduce* guests or other
speakers, and so forth.

In some speeches, more than one of these general purposes will need to overlap. It is difficult to imagine a successful persuasive speech that is not simultaneously highly informative, for example. On the other hand, it is important that superfluous objectives do not interfere with the primary purpose. For example, you have probably witnessed informative speeches in which the speaker tried so hard to entertain that the speech was of very little informative value to the audience.

In any case, it is useful to consider the broad purpose of a forthcoming speech, for this identifies the general "ballpark" of your communicative objectives. Much more important, however, is to identify a small number of *specific objectives*.

What Are Your Specific Objectives? As you begin to organize the speech content, it is useful, almost necessary in fact, to outline your main points and subpoints, much as you have been taught to outline written reports. But it is important that the outline be constructed with your *specific communicative objectives* well in mind. These specific primary objectives may or may not directly parallel the main "headings" on your outline.

By "specific communication objectives," I mean the two or three or so specific points you hope to have placed in the audience's minds by the end of the speech. A useful way to identify these objectives, especially for informative and persuasive speeches was alluded to earlier: Imagine a hypothetical quiz that you would like to give to the audience, after your speech, to find out whether they have understood and retained the main ideas and concepts you wanted them to. The three or so questions you would put on this hypothetical quiz represent your specific communicative objectives. Now, *planning the speech content becomes a matter of ensuring that the audience would be able to "ace" your hypothetical quiz*, for that would show that you have achieved your objectives.

When considering this hypothetical quiz it is important to be critical and ask whether achieving those objectives will indeed be of value to the audience. Can the large majority of the audience already answer your hypothetical quiz? If so, you may wish to revise one or more of the objectives toward newer and fresher ideas. Will it be of value *to the audience* if the objectives are achieved? If so, then the ways in which it is valuable may be useful as rationales in introducing certain points. And, of course, if you are not confident that the information is of value then you probably should revise your specific objectives. The same sort of double-checking should be done for persuasion objectives. Does the majority of the audience already believe or behave as your objectives intend? Do you sincerely believe that it is advantageous to the audience that they alter their beliefs or behaviors as your objectives intend? And so forth. In short, ensure that your specific objectives are valid objectives.

It is helpful also to remember that a typical speech should have relatively *few* specific objectives, and that each objective is reasonably "doable"—that is, not too ambitious

—within the time allotted for the speech. As a rough guide, one to three specific objectives is about right for 5 - 30 minute speeches, and three or four specific objectives is about right for 30 - 45 minute speeches. You may find this to be a remarkably low target. After all, you will be able to make a lot more than three or four points in a 30-minute speech. But part of the key to successful speech content is to make certain that all of the many *things* you will say during the speech are designed as illustration, explanation, exemplification, reinforcement, clarification, justification, amplification, and so forth, for a *very few primary points* you want the audience to grasp and remember.

To focus on a very few specific objectives—just a few questions on your hypothetical quiz—is one more way in which you may simultaneously improve the speech while reducing anxiety. The improvement in the speech comes from the fact that speakers who have not identified a few main objectives usually give unfocused speeches. They haven't determined the communicative relationship between the various parts of the speech, tend to treat all of the parts as equally weighted, and "lose" the audience who is trying to put it all together. The reduction in anxiety comes from the intuitive confidence that it is easier to be thorough, clear, and effective on a few specific objectives than on many.

CLARITY AND UNDERSTANDABILITY

There are two particular audience reactions that the commmunication-oriented speaker should wish to avoid.

One goes something like this: "Listening to that speech wasn't worthwhile. I understood what the speaker was saying, but I just didn't get anything new out of it." The main key to avoiding this response lies in the speaker's prior identification and scrutiny of the specific objectives, including an assessment of their value to the audience, as we discussed a moment ago.

The other reaction to avoid is the one that goes like this: "I didn't *understand* that speech. I really wanted to, because it seemed interesting and valuable, but I just couldn't follow it." It is, of course, vital that the audience understand the speech. Not that every member will understand every single example and detail, necessarily; but it is crucial that the large majority of the audience understands the large majority of the speech well enough that you achieve your main objectives with most of the audience.

For most speakers, the key to clarity is simply to make a considerable effort when planning the speech, keeping in mind the ways in which the audience is at a disadvantage: they don't know the same information that the speaker does, they don't know where the speech is going with respect to its objectives or its organization, they don't know which points are main points, subpoints, examples, illustrations, and so forth. There is much about the content which, although very clear to the speaker, cannot possibly be clear to the audience unless the speaker makes it clear for them. As speakers, we must put ourselves in the audience's shoes while preparing the speech, and from *their* perspective try to make what is clear to us clear to them.

To put it another way, we need to be concerned with clarity not only with respect to the individual statements we make, but also with respect to how those statements relate to one another. It isn't enough to show the audience the individual "trees." We need also to ensure, within reason, that they see the "forest," the "sections" of the forest, the "map" of the forest, and the "routes" used to get from one section to the next. Here are a few general guidelines that can be helpful toward ensuring clarity:

1. Let the Audience Know Where You're Going. Just as you will find it helpful to identify for yourself the specific objectives of the speech, the audience will usually find it helpful to know these objectives. They usually will appreciate knowing your rationale for these objectives as well.

A mistake that speakers sometimes make is to leave the audience wondering what the speaker is trying to accomplish. It is as if the speaker is giving the audience a smorgasbord from which they have to make their own guesses with respect to what is supposed to matter most. Rarely is this approach effective. Usually it is better to make clear to the audience what it is that the speaker wants to accomplish. This can be done in any of a variety of ways, including previewing the objectives at the beginning of the speech, flagging the objectives at relevant points in the speech, asking the person who introduces you to preview the objectives, and so on.

Along the same lines, speakers sometimes are reluctant to preview where the speech is going, out of concern that they will "give away," or tip off, the audience to some point that would be more effective as a surprise. This is a dangerous strategy. Usually the audience can follow you better if they have a good idea of where you are trying to go *before* you get there.

2. Don't Overload the Audience. Another common mistake by beginning speakers is "information overload" — expecting the audience to process and digest more than they can handle easily. It is important to recognize, as mentioned a moment ago, that the audience is at a communicative disadvantage. As audience members, they are receivers in a mostly one-way communication situation. While *you may* behave much as in natural conversation, *they may not.* They can't interrupt, ask for clarification, ask you to repeat yourself, put their two-cents worth in, or do many of the other things that listeners in conversation do when they miss, or fail to understand, or disagree with, something we say. Moreover, the speech audience is receiving information in "transient time." Unlike the hypothetical receiver who might read a transcript of a speech, or listen to one on audio tape, the live audience can neither glance back a few paragraphs to reread, nor hit the rewind button to rehear, when they become confused or lost. In short, to be in a speech audience is inherently one of the most difficult modes one can possibly be in as a communication receiver. The threshold for information overload is much lower than in most other communication situations, and the speaker needs to keep these limitations well in mind while preparing the speech.

3.   Use Organizational Markers. Imagine any clearly-written lengthy report or article you may have read recently, and think of all of the visual markers that were used to highlight the organization of the material—main section headings, sub-section headings, paragraph indentations, "bullets," and so forth. Now notice that since the voice is an acoustic medium, none of these familiar visual organization cues are available to the audience of a speech. True, your outline or your notes may have bullets, headings at various levels of subordination, and so forth. But, of course, your audience doesn't have your outline.

Since the audience can't *see* the organization, the speaker must "show" them the organization with spoken equivalents of paragraph indentations, section headings, bullets, and so forth. There are various ways to do this.

One crucial step is to *identify main points as main points*. Even if the speaker has tried to avoid information overload by reducing the main points to a very few, the audience will not necessarily know which points are main points unless the speaker identifies them as such. Since the main points are those around which the various parts of the speech are constructed, the audience will have trouble following the speaker if they don't know what these anchors are.

Similarly, it is helpful to *identify the function of subpoints, examples, and illustrations.* You probably can recall having heard a speech in which something that you assumed was a new point turned out to have been intended as an example of an earlier point. And there are cases where we are fairly certain that we are hearing an example, but are not certain which point it is supposed to be exemplifying. Likewise with illustrations, subpoints, analogies, contrasts, and other units of the speech. When preparing the speech, it is crucial that each small unit of the speech has, for the speaker, a specific communicative role to play. Next, it becomes crucial that the audience "sees" the intended role of each unit when the speech is delivered. This makes the speech much easier to follow.

It is crucial also to *use transitions* to let the audience know when you are finished with one matter and are moving on to another. Otherwise, when you begin discussing "Y," they will by trying to make sense of it in terms of "X" that you had been discussing before.

As an example of the level of organizational clarity that can be achieved with ample transitions, clear identifications of examples, main points, etc., I remember an assignment that I tried a few years ago. The students gave speeches which were tape recorded and later transcribed. The transcription of each speech was then separated into its various sub-parts (about 15 to 25 very short sections for these five-minute speeches), with the help of several assistants. Then we jumbled the subparts, and asked other students who had not heard the speeches to try to rearrange them back into their original form. For most of the speeches, this was impossible. But a few of the speeches had so clearly identified the function of their parts that they could actually be reconstructed. Of course, it isn't necessary that the audience be able to reassemble randomly jumbled parts of your speech. But it is worth keeping in mind the level of organizational clarity that can be achieved when the audience understands the function you intend for each part of the speech.

For slightly different reasons, it is valuable also to identify and differentiate between facts and suppositions, true situations and hypothetical situations, original ideas and borrowed ideas, and so forth. This is helpful for clarity, since the audience will be distracted if they need to wonder which is which. And it is helpful for credibility if they already know or suspect which is which.

In short, preparing the speech content is like solving a puzzle. The puzzle begins with the audience members' minds in their pre-speech state, and the destination is for those minds to know, understand, and accept that which is indicated by your specific communicative objectives. To solve the puzzle involves making wise choices about the steps needed to take their minds from where they are now to where you want them to be after the speech. The challenge is to ensure that those steps are successful, and the trick is to make a serious effort for clarity at every point along the way.

BACK TO THE MATTER OF ANXIETY

To discuss speech content within our larger discussion of speech anxiety presents an ostensible paradox. On the one hand, we've been saying that there is no need for anxiety about performance-oriented concerns, because the goal of the speech is to achieve communication objectives, very much as in everyday conversation. One the other hand, our discussion of content suggests that the achievement of these communicative objectives should not be taken lightly. It may seem that we have simply replaced a set of performance-oriented anxieties with a new set of communication-oriented concerns. In a way, I suppose that this is true. But it certainly does *not* put you back where you started with respect to public-speaking anxiety, because communication-oriented concerns are easier to satisfy than performance-oriented concerns. The criteria are clearer, and what is needed to satisfy the criteria is within the control of the speaker.

Before the speech, you *should* feel communication-oriented pressure — pressure to prepare the content, prepare more, and prepare still more, in order to be confident that you will achieve your specific objectives. This will, most likely, take a few hours of formal planning, where you sit with pen and paper to map out your content strategies. And it will likely occupy a fair amount of casual time, where you reflect on new points and new ways of making certain points while driving, showering, washing dishes, and so forth. But the payoff for the pre-speech pressure is that you go into the speech with confidence that you know what you want to say. And by now, you should have confidence that saying it will be relatively easy. Presumably, your efforts in planning the content will culminate in a sketchy outline, or cryptic notes, to remind you of the order in which you want to make certain points. Again, the delivery of the speech will be a simple matter of telling the audience what you have *planned* to tell them.

As for your concern over whether the content has indeed been well-planned, here are two pieces of reassurance for you:

First, this is exactly where your concern should be directed. It shows a communication-oriented conscientiousness that leads to better, and more anxiety-free, speeches. Secondly, if you find yourself concerned about content, it probably means that you will do fine with respect to communicative objectives. This is because those who don't succeed communicatively are not those who were concerned, tried, and failed, but rather are almost always those who never paid serious attention to communication-oriented goals in the first place. It is almost always the case that if the speaker has been concerned or preoccupied with content matters, then the content ends up being remarkably good, and the communicative objectives end up being met. That is why this chapter has been brief and general. I have seen over and over that poor content does not come from an *inability* to organize, plan, analyze the audience, strategize, clarify, and so forth. Rather, it comes from the simple absence of serious effort. Some speakers, for example, will assume that the first organization that intuitively comes to mind will suffice. Others will assume that the organization of the written reports on which the speech is based can be borrowed directly for the speech. And others will take other short-cuts without seriously questioning and developing their speech content with their particular target audience in mind. These are the speeches that usually are ineffective.

Again, when content fails, it is almost always because hardly any effort was expended by the speaker to adapt the content to his or her primary objectives. I am confident in saying that once a communication-oriented speaker has been concerned about content, has expended a reasonable effort to optimize the content with respect to specific objectives for a specific audience, and approaches the speech with those objectives in mind, there is very little need to be anxious about content (or anything else) at the time of the actual speech.

CHAPTER 6

A REVIEW OF KEY THEMES

If you are like most readers of this handbook, you are much more confident and relaxed about giving speeches now than you were when we began. You probably can feel the difference. And if you like, you can retake the questionnaire you completed in Chapter 2. I've put another copy of the questionnaire at the end of this chapter. In addition to the subjective feeling of greater confidence, you will probably see "objective" evidence of improvement as well.

Our mission is virtually complete. As a final touch, let's briefly review a few of the underlying themes that have emerged throughout our discussion.

1. Understanding the Phenomenon of Public-Speaking Anxiety

We noticed early in our discussion that several facts about public-speaking anxiety are worth keeping in mind when dealing with it. For example, it is sometimes comforting to know that public-speaking anxiety is very common and pervasive in our culture. The anxiety you had when we began was not all that unusual. What you probably will be experiencing in the future is normal or even lower than normal. That is worth keeping in mind. It is useful also to know about the natural pattern that public-speaking anxiety follows before and during the speech. The "anticipation reaction" just before the speech, and the more powerful "confrontation reaction" that occurs when you first begin the speech, should be remembered and expected. Even though they presumably will be much less intense for your future speeches than they have been in the past, do expect some version of them so that they do not take you by surprise and cause undue alarm. And the "adaptation reaction"— the natural diminishing of anxiety after the speech begins —should be remembered and recognized so that you can capitalize on it.

2. The Performance Orientation and Public-Speaking Anxiety

An important part of understanding the anxiety phenomenon is understanding its origin. We have followed a theory by which a "performance orientation" to public speaking sets in motion a cycle of physiological arousal (increased heart rate, sweaty palms, etc.) and psychological interpretations (usually "fear" and its "causes"). The performance orientation is inherently anxiety-arousing in several ways. It assumes (incorrectly) that speeches primarily involve evaluation and close scrutiny by the audience; and the idea of being evaluated and scrutinized is almost always anxiety-arousing. It also assumes (incorrectly) that novel, formal, or otherwise unfamiliar behaviors are required. Again, situations where we are expected to be overly formal, or where we don't know how we are supposed to act, almost always induce anxiety.

3. Real Speeches are Not Like Most Classroom Speeches

If the performance orientation is ill-founded and counter-productive, then why do so many speakers have this orientation? Throughout our discussion we have seen several ways in which our grade school and high school public-speaking experiences probably contributed to a performance orientation. More importantly, we have seen several ways in which real-life speeches are very different from our early classroom experiences. Unlike many classroom speeches, where the class and/or the teacher already knows the material we are presenting, real-life audiences do not. Similarly, unlike classmates who often are not truly interested in listening to classmates' speeches, our real-life audiences generally are there because they want to hear what we have to say. Unlike classmates who fixate on delivery quirks—counting our "uh's" and the like —mature audiences fix on the information. Unlike classroom speeches where the requirement or advice (implicit or explicit) was to memorize the speech, real-life audiences abhor memorized-sounding speeches, and prefer a more natural, direct style. And unlike classroom speeches where the feedback and the grading criteria focused on a checklist of speaker's behaviors, the primary criterion in real-life speeches is the audience's comprehension and acquisition of information. In all of these contrasts, the classroom experience feeds the performance orientation to public speaking, which in turn feeds anxiety for most speakers. The real-life contrast in each case suggests an alternative orientation, however.

4. The Communication Orientation to Public Speaking

The alternative is, of course, what I have called the "communication orientation." As was implied earlier, my primary objective all along has been to persuade you to adopt this alternative orientation, since it forms the basis both for reduced anxiety and improved speeches. Essentially, the communication orientation is a view by which the primary objective of the speech is to achieve certain *communication* goals rather than performance goals. By "communication goals" we mean especially getting your main points across to the audience. If that is accomplished, little else matters.

5. We Already Know How Because We Give Many Mini-Speeches Every Day

As we have seen over and over, the communication orientation simultaneously promotes reduced anxiety and improves speech quality. One of the main ways it reduces anxiety is by recognizing that, for the most part, giving a speech is very much like any serious conversation that we have in our everyday lives. The objectives are the same — namely, sharing our thoughts and getting our points across to someone else. We accomplish these goals in everyday conversation, so there is part of the proof that we are capable of doing what is required of a speech. Moreover, the communication behaviors that we use in conversation — the speaking style, gestures, expression, and so forth — are the same behaviors that are most effective in public speaking. So again, since we know how to converse, we already know how to give a speech.

To put it another way, the ideal delivery style is characterized by directness, and directness is most effectively achieved with well-planned yet spontaneous and non-scripted talk that parallels the way we talk in everyday conversation. Once again, as for whether we "have what it takes" to give a good speech, there are innumerable ways in which we already do exactly what it takes practically every day.

Indeed, there are very few differences between serious conversation and public speaking. The few differences that *do* exist are viewed, from a communication perspective, as *advantages* to public speaking: We get to share our information with more listeners at once, we get to talk longer without being interrupted, and we get to plan more carefully and more thoroughly before we start talking.

6. Recognize How You React as an Audience Member

It is almost certain that as a high-anxiety speaker, you had a performance orientation to public speaking. And, obviously, I have tried to persuade you to shift to a communication orientation. As for why you should agree to switch, I am hoping that you believe the various points I have made about the advantages of the communication perspective — advantages both in terms of reducing anxiety and in terms of improving your speeches. But, as we have seen at several places in our discussion, you don't have to simply take my word for it. You can see for yourself that the communication orientation makes sense by noticing and reflecting on you own reactions to speakers and speeches when *you* are in the *audience*.

You will agree, I think, that you and other audience members assume an overall communication perspective. Mature audiences simply do not scrutinize and evaluate speakers on performance skills like Olympic figure-skating judges or like sixth-grade teachers who grade speeches with delivery check-lists.   Instead, audiences listen to, and try to understand, what is being said.   This is what you do in an audience, and this is what your audience will do during your speeches.   Likewise, I am confident that as an audience member you appreciate sincere, direct, and natural speakers more than robotic speakers with scripted speeches.   And I'm sure that you feel a "connection" to speakers who may never make eye contact with you in particular, but are "connecting" by seeing and talking to other individuals in the audience.   And I'll bet that you appreciate most the speakers from whom you gained the most information with the least amount of effort. And so on. For virtually all of the implicit and explicit advice I have given with respect to taking a communication orientation, you don't have to just take my word for it. You can confirm it with your own experience as an audience member of others' speeches.

7. Focus on Content

Delivery, the aspect of public speaking which most concerns the performance-oriented speaker, turns out to be very easy with a communication orientation The communication-oriented speaker recognizes that the style used in everyday talk is precisely what works best in public speaking, recognizes that speeches do not call for overly formal or otherwise novel delivery behaviors or standards, and recognizes that delivery behaviors are not where the audience's attention is focused anyway. From a communication perspective, what used to be imagined as the hard part turns out to be the easy part.

But while taking comfort in learning that delivery is much easier than we once thought, it is important to recognize that giving a good speech is still a challenge. The challenge is in preparing the content before giving the speech. The communication orientation reminds us of this by the way in which it establishes the criteria for an effective speech: *A speech is a good speech to the extent that it achieves its communicative purpose.* We have seen, for example, that some college instructors determine speech grades on the basis of quizzes over what the audience learned from the speeches they heard. And we have seen that imagining a hypothetical quiz of this sort is a good way for speakers to focus clearly on their specific communication objectives. Once these objectives are identified by the speaker, the "bad news" is that preparing the content to ensure achieving these objectives takes time and work. The "good news" is that communication-oriented speakers tend to take this task seriously, and thus are more successful in knowing and achieving their communication objectives.

8. There is Nothing to Fear

Part of the physical/psychological cycle that characterizes public-speaking anxiety is the interpretation of physical symptoms as fear, and then justifying that interpretation by finding things to be afraid of in the speech. What we have seen throughout our discussion, however—explicitly in Chapter 3 and implicitly elsewhere—is that the fears identified by high-anxiety speakers are groundless. Common fears, for example, are "the audience will ridicule me if I make a mistake," "I'll make a fool of myself," "I have to be formal," "the audience will be scrutinizing my every move," "the audience will detect my anxiety," and so forth. In all of these cases, our discussion has shown these fears to be based on assumptions that simply are not true.

YOUR NEXT FEW SPEECHES

The anxiety-reduction program we have just completed seems to work extremely well when one's next speech follows within a few days. When the first communication-oriented speech is within a week or so of finishing the book, the speaker usually experiences a very substantial reduction in anxiety compared to past speeches, and the anxiety subsides even further in subsequent speeches—especially if they are given within a month or so of each other. So, if your next speech is coming up fairly soon, you are probably "ready" as far as anxiety reduction is concerned.   Likewise, if subsequent speeches follow fairly frequently.

But if your next speech is further in the future, or if your subsequent speeches are further apart, you may wish to refresh your memory and your communication orientation by reviewing this book as the speech date approaches.   I would suggest rereading or reviewing at least Chapters 2 and 3 about a week before your next speech, and within three weeks or so of the next speech after that one.   Within two or three speeches with this new approach fresh on your mind, you will likely "hit stride" as a communication-oriented speaker, and your successes will be all the reminder you need on subsequent speeches.

I wish you well on your future speeches, of course.   I hope that your audiences leave satisfied that they understood what you were saying.   And I hope you leave satisfied that the audience's time listening to you was time well spent— for them and for you.

A GAUGE OF PUBLIC-SPEAKING ANXIETY*

DIRECTIONS: <u>Assume that you have to give a speech within the next few weeks</u>. For each of the statements below, indicate the degree to which the statement applies to you, within the context of giving a future speech. Mark whether you strongly agree (SA), agree (A), are undecided (U), disagree (D), or strongly disagree (SD) with each statement. Circle the SA, A, U, D, SD choices. Don't write in the blanks next to the questions. *Work quickly; just record your first impression.*

___1. While preparing for the speech I would feel uncomfortably tense and nervous. SA_5 A_4 U_3 D_2 SD_1

___2. I feel uncomfortably tense at the very thought of giving a speech in the near future. SA_5 A_4 U_3 D_2 SD_1

___3. My thoughts would become confused and jumbled when I was giving a speech. SA_5 A_4 U_3 D_2 SD_1

___4. Right after giving the speech I would feel that I'd had a pleasant experience. SA_1 A_2 U_3 D_4 SD_5

___5. I would get anxious when thinking about the speech coming up. SA_5 A_4 U_3 D_2 SD_1

___6. I would have no fear of giving the speech. SA_1 A_2 U_3 D_4 SD_5

___7. Although I would be nervous just before starting the speech, after starting it I would soon settle down and feel calm and comfortable. SA_1 A_2 U_3 D_4 SD_5

___8. I would look forward to giving the speech. SA_1 A_2 U_3 D_4 SD_5

___9. As soon as I knew that I would have to give the speech, I would feel myself getting tense. SA_5 A_4 U_3 D_2 SD_1

___10. My hands would tremble when I SA_5 A_4 U_3 D_2 SD_1
        am giving the speech.

___11. I would feel relaxed while giving SA_1 A_2 U_3 D_4 SD_5
        the speech.

___12. I would enjoy preparing for the SA_1 A_2 U_3 D_4 SD_5
        speech.

___13. I would be in constant fear of SA_5 A_4 U_3 D_2 SD_1
        forgetting what I had prepared to
        say.

___14. I would get uncomfortably anxious SA_5 A_4 U_3 D_2 SD_1
        if someone asked me something
        that I did not know about my topic.

___15. I would face the prospect of giving SA_1 A_2 U_3 D_4 SD_5
        the speech with confidence.

___16. I would feel that I was in complete SA_1 A_2 U_3 D_4 SD_5
        possession of myself during the
        speech.

___17. My mind would be clear when SA_1 A_2 U_3 D_4 SD_5
        giving the speech.

___18. I would not dread giving the speech. SA_1 A_2 U_3 D_4 SD_5

___19. I would perspire too much just before SA_5 A_4 U_3 D_2 SD_1
        starting the speech.

___20. I would be bothered by a very fast SA_5 A_4 U_3 D_2 SD_1
        heart rate just as I started the speech.

___21. I would experience considerable SA_5 A_4 U_3 D_2 SD_1
        anxiety at the speech site (room,
        auditorium, etc.) just before my speech
        was to start.

___22. Certain parts of my body would feel SA_5 A_4 U_3 D_2 SD_1
        very tense and rigid during the speech.

___23. Realizing that only a little time SA_5 A_4 U_3 D_2 SD_1
        remained in the speech would make
        me very tense and anxious.

___24. While giving the speech I would SA_1 A_2 U_3 D_4 SD_5
        know that I could control my
        feelings of tension and stress.

___25. I would breathe too fast just before SA_5 A_4 U_3 D_2 SD_1
        starting the speech.

__26. I would feel comfortable and relaxed in the hour or so just before giving the speech. $SA_1 \ A_2 \ U_3 \ D_4 \ SD_5$

__27. I would do poorly on speech because I would be anxious. $SA_5 \ A_4 \ U_3 \ D_2 \ SD_1$

__28. I would feel uncomfortably anxious when first scheduling the date of the speaking engagement. $SA_5 \ A_4 \ U_3 \ D_2 \ SD_1$

__29. If I were to make a mistake while giving the speech, I would find it hard to concentrate on the parts that followed. $SA_5 \ A_4 \ U_3 \ D_2 \ SD_1$

__30. During the speech I would experience a feeling of helplessness building up inside me. $SA_5 \ A_4 \ U_3 \ D \ SD_1$

__31. I would have trouble falling asleep the night before the speech. $SA_5 \ A_4 \ U_3 \ D_2 \ SD_1$

__32. My heart would beat too fast while I presented the speech. $SA_5 \ A_4 \ U_3 \ D_2 \ SD_1$

__33. I would feel uncomfortably anxious while waiting to give my speech. $SA_5 \ A_4 \ U_3 \ D_2 \ SD_1$

__34. While giving the speech I would get so nervous I would forget facts I really know. $SA_5 \ A_4 \ U_3 \ D_2 \ SD_1$

____(TOTAL)

To determine your anxiety score:

1. Fill in the blank next to each "question" with the NUMBER printed with the response you circled. BE CAREFUL to enter the CORRECT NUMBER. NOTICE that the numbers printed with the responses are not consistent for every question.
2. Add up the numbers you recorded for the 34 questions. The sum is your anxiety score.

INTERPRETATION

SCORE	PUBLIC-SPEAKING ANXIETY LEVEL
34-84	Low
85-92	Moderately Low
93-110	Moderate
111-119	Moderately High
120-170	High

NOTE: About 95% of anxious speakers who complete the program in this book experience a substantial reduction in public-speaking anxiety. If you are one of the few who does not, then you may wish to reread the material or to contact a therapist for an alternate treatment program, such as the ones described in Chapter 1.

*Adapted from James C. McCroskey's "Personal Report of Public Speaking Anxiety," as presented in J. McCroskey, "Measures of Communication-Bound Anxiety," Speech Monographs, vol. 37.4, p. 276. Used by permission of the Speech Communication Association.

BIBLIOGRAPHY

The sources cited below were the most direct references used in this book. I did not usually cite them explicitly in the discussion, partly to simplify the reading, and partly because I rarely presented information having only a single source. In any case, I am grateful to these and other scholars in the fields of communication and psychology who have made valuable discoveries and insights regarding the speech-anxiety phenomenon.

Beatty, M. J. & Behnke, R. R. (1991). Effects of public speaking trait anxiety and intensity of speaking task on heart rate during performance. *Human Communication Research, 18*, 147-176.

Behnke, R. R. & Beatty, M. J. (1981). A cognitive-physiological model of speech anxiety. *Communication Monographs, 48*, 158-163.

Behnke, R. R. & Carlile, L. W. (1971). Heart rate as an index of speech anxiety. *Speech Monographs, 38*, 65-69.

Clevenger, T. (1959). A synthesis of experimental research in stage fright. *Quarterly Journal of Speech, 45*, 134-145.

Clevenger, T., Motley, M. T. & Carlile, L. W. (1967). *Changes in heart rate during classroom public speaking.* Unpublished manuscript, University of Texas, Austin.

Daly, J. A. & McCroskey, J. C. (1984). (Eds.) *Avoiding communication: Shyness, reticence, and communication apprehension.* Beverly Hills: Sage.

Fremouw, W. J. (1984). Cognitive-behavioral therapies for modification of communication apprehension. In J.A. Daly and J. C. McCroskey (eds.), *Avoiding communication: Shyness, reticence, and communication apprehension.* Beverly Hills: Sage.

McCroskey, J. C. (1970). Measures of communication-bound anxiety. *Speech Monographs, 37,* 269-277.

Motley, M. T. (1988). Taking the terror out of talk. *Psychology Today, 22, 1,* 46-49.

Motley, M. T. (1990). Public speaking anxiety qua performance anxiety: A revised model and an alternative therapy. *Journal of Social Behavior and Personality, 5,* 85-104.

Motley, M. T. & Molloy, J. L. (1994). An efficacy test of a new therapy ("Communication-Orientation Motivation") for public speaking anxiety. *Journal of Applied Communication Research, 22,* 48-58.

Richmond, V. P. & McCroskey, J. C. (1985). *Communication: Apprehension, avoidance, and effectiveness.* Scottsdale, AZ: Gorsuch Scarisbrick.